WILLIAM CHAPMAN WALLER
(1850-1917)

LOUGHTON'S HISTORIAN

William Chapman Waller 1850-1917
(Portrait by D Radcliffe-Beresford 1916)

William Chapman Waller
(1850-1917)

Loughton's Historian

by

Richard Morris, OBE
Verderer of Epping Forest

LOUGHTON
THE LOUGHTON AND DISTRICT HISTORICAL SOCIETY
2001

ISBN 0952 88055 5

Production by
Ted Martin
Theydon Bois, Essex CM16 7JX

Typeset and designed by
Artform
Little Tew, Oxfordshire OX7 4JH

Printed in Great Britain by
The Lavenham Press
Lavenham, Suffolk

PREFACE

In reading about Loughton, Epping Forest and Essex I had for many years come across footnotes quoting William Waller as a source and in particular his book *Loughton in Essex*. It was almost by chance when I was scanning the catalogue at the Guildhall Library in the City of London for items of interest on Epping Forest, that I found that they had one of the twelve bound copies of the book. Visits to the British Library and Essex Record Office soon showed how important had been Waller's contribution to documenting the history of Loughton and Essex.

Thanks to the continuing link that the Waller family has with the Whitaker Almshouses in Loughton, I was able to make contact with William Waller's granddaughter and great granddaughter, who have been able to provide much information about the man himself and his family.

In deciding what to include in this memoir I was conscious that much of Waller's work is hidden away in the libraries of national institutions and societies and at county level. It is one of the penalties of historical and archaeological research that its results are often buried away, only rarely to be seen again by the new historian. Many of Waller's articles are certainly worthy of being reprinted. I have therefore tried to provide a taste of the wide range of Waller's work by quoting in some detail from his more important contributions, as well as trying to assess their importance.

One of the difficulties faced by the historian in referring to place names and people is that often, over the centuries, a different form of spelling is used. Without wishing to confuse the reader I have used the forms relevant to the period of time about which I am writing. My only defence is that I am following Waller in this practice.

I have received much help and encouragement from many people in researching this slim volume. I must first thank Diana Waller, granddaughter, and Anna Row, great granddaughter for their help. Many visits to the Essex Record Office were always productive, as were visits to other libraries and institutions with which Waller had contact. I apologise for not naming them all. Nearer to home the support of the Loughton and District Historical Society and in particular Chris Pond has been invaluable.

Loughton, September 2000   RICHARD MORRIS

Above: W C Waller with groom, pony and trap at Ash Green
Below: W C Waller's favourite horse: 'Ruby', with groom (1906)

CONTENTS

Lilium auratum at Ash Green in 1904

ILLUSTRATIONS

1
FROM WESTMORLAND TO LOUGHTON

Although the main purpose of this memoir is to assess the literary and academic work of William Chapman Waller, as a local and county antiquarian and historian, a note on the man himself and his family is necessary if Waller's contribution to the community is to be fully appreciated.

In researching the family history, this can be divided into three periods. First, the origins of the Wallers in the early seventeenth century in the Eden Valley in Westmorland. Second is the period about which very little information appears to be available and covers the time from the second half of the eighteenth century when the first William Waller, son of Edward Waller of Thorny Gaile, came down from Westmorland to London, up to Jane Miller Waller's move to Loughton in about 1870. This includes the first twenty years of William Chapman Waller's life. The third period covers life at Ash Green from 1870 until Waller's death in July 1917, and for which there is much information both in writing and a photographic record, the latter in the main thanks to Waller's wife.

WESTMORLAND

Waller prepared, with the assistance of the College of Arms, a pedigree of his line of the family, going back as far as 1609. The pedigree shown on page 7 identifies Thomas Waller living at the beginning of the seventeenth century at High Ewbanke in the parish of Brough in Westmorland. High Ewbanke is still shown today on the Ordnance Survey map and lies about three miles south east of Brough in the northern Pennines and east of the Eden valley. A son, also called Thomas, was born in December 1614 and subsequently lived at Thorny Gaile which lies between High Ewbanke and Brough.

Family legend is that the Wallers in Westmorland were yeomen farmers. This was a common description for occupations appearing in the wills of people who lived in Cumbria in the seventeenth century. A yeoman indicates someone who has an estate and is independent but there can be a very wide divergence of wealth of individual yeomen. The parish of Brough was in the diocese of Carlisle and wills proved in the Consistory Court of Carlisle between 1661 and 1750 include those for a Thomas Waller of Thorny Gaile in 1665 and another Thomas Waller also of Thorny Gaile whose will was proved in 1748. The two wills describe the deceased as yeomen and, bearing in mind that Thorny Gaile was a very small hamlet, seem likely to refer to the two Wallers shown in William Chapman Waller's pedigree as dying in 1665 and 1748, although in the first case the speed for proving the will would have been unusually quick.

LONDON

Another three generations of Wallers were to live at Thorny Gaile before the first William Waller, who was baptised in July 1763, came to live in London. This member of the Waller family died in Hackney in 1803 at the age of 40. His wife Elizabeth, *née* Miller, lived until 1853. They had two children: William Miller Waller of Fairford House in Hackney, who was born in 1797, and Jane Miller Waller born in 1800.

William Miller Waller married Ann Elizabeth Chapman in December 1848 at St Philip's Church in Dalston and they had two children: William Chapman Waller, born at Hackney on 27 August 1850 and Jane Elizabeth born in October 1851. From this we can see that Jane Miller Waller was William Chapman Waller's aunt. The occupation of William Chapman Waller's father is described as a 'Gentleman' but Waller's grandfather is shown on his father's marriage certificate as a 'woollen draper'.

We now move forward twenty years to 1870 or 1871, when the census shows Jane Miller Waller as a visitor to Loughton staying at Ash Green with the then occupant Eliza Watson. It is believed that Eliza Watson had been a school friend of Jane Miller Waller. Eliza Watson *née* Lane, had been born in Marylebone in 1803, not far from Jane Miller Waller, who was born at St Mary le Strand, Middlesex.

LOUGHTON

Eliza Watson had moved to Loughton with her father Charles Lane, a doctor, and of whom we will hear more later, in about 1807 and had inherited the house at Ash Green from him on his death. Eliza had married William Watson, who was to become the curate at St John's Church in Loughton, and lived at first in the cottage, originally known as Bigg's cottage, in the grounds of Ash Green, until her father died. William Watson died in 1869 and it appears that Jane Miller Waller, who herself had never married, came to live with her widowed friend. The Watsons had no children and Eliza only lived for two years after her husband's death. We therefore find that Eliza Watson, after a number of bequests to hospitals for the poor and the incurable, left her remaining estate including the house at Ash Green and most of its contents, together with other property in Loughton, to Jane Miller Waller.

Little if anything is known of the first twenty years of William Chapman Waller's life. His father had died when his son was only four years of age, and his mother died when he was twenty-four years old. It is not clear whether his parents were well off, but it would not appear so from his mother's will. This may account for the suggestion that William Chapman Waller's aunt Jane effectively adopted him in 1874 and subsequently paid for his education. This would also explain why Waller appears to have been a 'mature' student, not graduating from University College, Oxford, until he was thirty years old.

The only other reference that we have to Waller's earlier education is in 1871 when a prize was awarded to him by the Department of General Literature and Science at King's College, London. The prize was for Modern History and is perhaps the first indication of Waller's interest in the subject which was to occupy him for the next 46 years. There is no reference to Waller graduating from King's College, London, but this was not unusual at this time as students were often prepared for entrance to Oxford and Cambridge Universities.

Following his mother's death in 1874, it is likely that William Chapman Waller moved to Loughton to live with his aunt at Ash Green. How soon thereafter he started his studies at University College, Oxford is not known but he graduated in 1880. Two important events happened shortly thereafter. In 1881 he married Emma Massey Cooke. Emma was to be known by the family as 'Minnie'. Soon after William and Emma returned from their honeymoon, Jane Miller Waller, William's aunt, died.

Jane Miller Waller had become a wealthy lady by her inheritance and William Chapman Waller and his sister Jane Elizabeth were to inherit much of their aunt's estate. William Chapman Waller took over the house at Ash Green and was to live there until his death. We will see later how he altered and extended the house, developed the garden and bought other property.

A NEW FAMILY

Four years were to pass before the first of William and Minnie's children was born. A daughter, Evelyn, was born in 1885 and was to live at Ash Green for sixty years until her death in 1945. In 1887 a second daughter, Vera, was born. It seems likely that she was never a strong girl and she died in 1895 at the young age of eight years. William and Minnie arranged for a lych gate to be built at St John's Church, Loughton, in memory of Vera, and this remains today.

Tragedy was not to be new to the Wallers. In 1890 a son Geoffrey was born. At an early age he joined the Royal Navy as a midshipman but in 1908 was killed in an accident on board ship. There is a memorial brass to him in St John's Church at Loughton. In February 1892 a second son, Ambrose, was born. He was to have a distinguished career in the Essex Regiment and subsequently in public service as an Essex County Councillor and Chairman of the Stour River Catchment Board.

A GRANT OF ARMS

The assistance that Waller sought from the College of Arms in researching his family's pedigree may have been the result of his wish to apply for Letters Patent for a Grant of Arms. It appears that none of Waller's predecessors in his line of the family had a right of Arms. Waller set about researching the Arms used by other branches of the Waller family and together with the advice and approval of Bluemantle Pursuivant, he was in 1887 granted his own Arms. The Arms include a griffin between two saltires, and three walnut leaves, which in various forms are common to other Waller family Arms. Waller chose as his motto: *'Fide Sed Cui Vide',* which can be translated as: 'Trust, but in whom take care'. This was the motto of the Wroth family who lived at Loughton Hall and about whom Waller was to contribute much historical research.

FAMILY LIFE AND FRIENDS

In which year Waller started his law studies is not clear but the Census of 1891 describes him as an Inner Temple Student at Law. He was not called to the Bar until 1895 at the age of 45. It is believed that Waller never practised at the Bar.

A photographic record of life at Ash Green in the 1890s and later still exists. Many of the photographs were taken by Minnie Waller. They show family life, the development of the house at Ash Green and many views of Epping Forest and local buildings. With the substantial inheritance from his aunt, Waller was able to pursue his interests in archaeology and natural history. His legal training and attention to detail provided the basis for the comprehensive archive of his writings which we have today. Later in this memoir an assessment is made of his contributions to the Essex Field Club, the Essex Archaeological Society and the Huguenot Society. Nearer to home his active membership of the local church and other associations in Loughton are recorded. A small archive of some of his working papers is held at the Essex Record Office and again demonstrates his painstaking attention to detail.

Less academic, but still of importance, are the diaries which William Waller kept from 1904 to 1917 and which remain in the possession of his descendants. A further small leather-bound volume records his bicycle rides throughout Essex, Hertfordshire and further afield. His wife also recorded life at Ash Green from 1888 to 1905 during the formative years of her young family.

As a result of his varied interests Waller made many friends both locally and through his wider academic researches. The name William Minet appears regularly in his diaries and writings, not only as a result of their contributions to the Huguenot Society, but also simply as a friend whose families met and joined in bicycle rides in the countryside. Minet lived at Little Hadham in Hertfordshire. The Buxton family of Warlies, Woodridden and Knighton appear, mainly in connection with Epping Forest.

John Whitaker Maitland, who was both Lord of the Manor and Rector of St John's Church, formed a close friendship and was able to assist Waller by providing original documents for some of his local historical researches. Edward Wauhope lived at Goldings Manor and although he came from a background totally different to Waller, they had much in common in their acquisition of property in Loughton. The two families, parents and children, often met at each other's houses. H H Francis was an architect who had two sons of similar age to Geoffrey and Ambrose Waller, and a number of photographs show the four boys together.

Perhaps this side of Waller's character is best summed up in the bequest that he made in his will, of £5 to each of a dozen or more of his friends, 'wherewith to buy a Gold Signet Ring or some other such small memorial of the Friendship we had'.

Waller's wife Minnie was to live at Ash Green for another 22 years after her husband's death. The house was sold following Evelyn's death in 1945. Fortunately many items from the house during William Waller's time have remained in the possession of the family, including portraits of Jane Miller Waller and William Chapman Waller, together with items of furniture and porcelain.

THE WALLER PEDIGREE

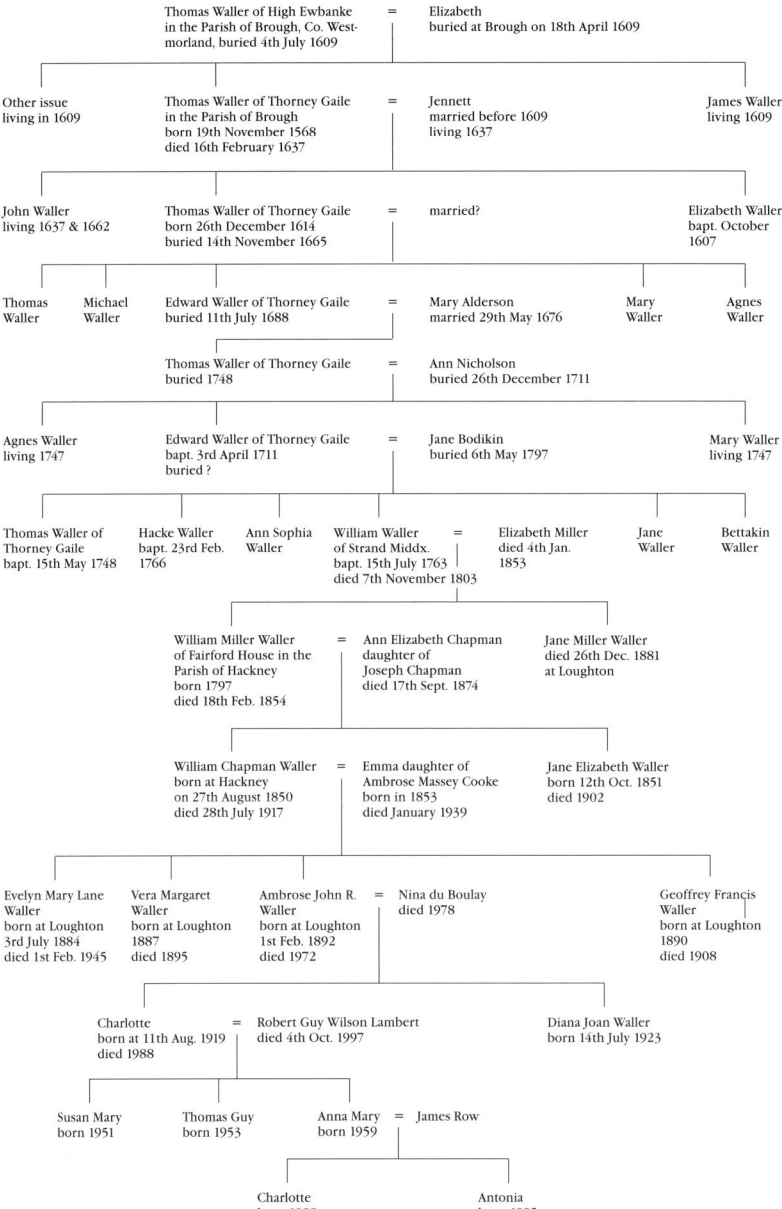

Thomas Waller of High Ewbanke in the Parish of Brough, Co. Westmorland, buried 4th July 1609 = Elizabeth buried at Brough on 18th April 1609

Other issue living in 1609

Thomas Waller of Thorney Gaile in the Parish of Brough born 19th November 1568 died 16th February 1637 = Jennett married before 1609 living 1637

James Waller living 1609

John Waller living 1637 & 1662

Thomas Waller of Thorney Gaile born 26th December 1614 buried 14th November 1665 = married?

Elizabeth Waller bapt. October 1607

Thomas Waller

Michael Waller

Edward Waller of Thorney Gaile buried 11th July 1688 = Mary Alderson married 29th May 1676

Mary Waller

Agnes Waller

Thomas Waller of Thorney Gaile buried 1748 = Ann Nicholson buried 26th December 1711

Agnes Waller living 1747

Edward Waller of Thorney Gaile bapt. 3rd April 1711 buried ? = Jane Bodikin buried 6th May 1797

Mary Waller living 1747

Thomas Waller of Thorney Gaile bapt. 15th May 1748

Hacke Waller bapt. 23rd Feb. 1766

Ann Sophia Waller

William Waller of Strand Middx. bapt. 15th July 1763 died 7th November 1803 = Elizabeth Miller died 4th Jan. 1853

Jane Waller

Bettakin Waller

William Miller Waller of Fairford House in the Parish of Hackney born 1797 died 18th Feb. 1854 = Ann Elizabeth Chapman daughter of Joseph Chapman died 17th Sept. 1874

Jane Miller Waller died 26th Dec. 1881 at Loughton

William Chapman Waller born at Hackney on 27th August 1850 died 28th July 1917 = Emma daughter of Ambrose Massey Cooke born in 1853 died January 1939

Jane Elizabeth Waller born 12th Oct. 1851 died 1902

Evelyn Mary Lane Waller born at Loughton 3rd July 1884 died 1st Feb. 1945

Vera Margaret Waller born at Loughton 1887 died 1895

Ambrose John R. Waller born at Loughton 1st Feb. 1892 died 1972 = Nina du Boulay died 1978

Geoffrey Francis Waller born at Loughton 1890 died 1908

Charlotte born at 11th Aug. 1919 died 1988 = Robert Guy Wilson Lambert died 4th Oct. 1997

Diana Joan Waller born 14th July 1923

Susan Mary born 1951

Thomas Guy born 1953

Anna Mary born 1959 = James Row

Charlotte born 1989

Antonia born 1995

Above: W C Waller at Loughton Horticultural Show in 1901
Below: Emma ('Minnie') Waller in garden of Ash Green in 1902

Above: W C Waller's sons Geoffrey and Ambrose with two friends in 1898
Below: Ambrose Waller near the 'old' Wheatsheaf in 1905

W C Waller's daughter Evelyn at Ash Green in 1903

Above: The four Waller children in 1885, with nurse and two friends
Below: W C Waller's sons, with sons of H Francis in 1906

Evelyn Waller in theatrical pose (c 1900)

2
ASH GREEN AND OTHER PROPERTY OWNED BY WALLER

ASH GREEN

It would no doubt please Waller to know that his house at Ash Green is today a Grade II listed building. Waller researched the history of the house and adjoining land and during his ownership he rebuilt and extended parts of the house. He would be less happy to know that today his garden is only one third of its original size, as two small housing developments were built at the beginning of the 1980s on the north eastern and southern parts of his land.

Waller refers to the history of Ash Green and how the land was acquired through the consolidation of various small enclosures, in both his book *Loughton in Essex* and his manuscript *An Itinerary of Loughton.* This provides an interesting insight into the history of this part of Loughton and its inhabitants of the nineteenth and early twentieth centuries. I can do no better than to quote an extract from *An Itinerary of Loughton* which Waller wrote in December 1911. I have added some clarifications in italics.

'The nucleus *[of the land at Ash Green]* was the cottage and orchard late in the tenure of George Woolard and now of Thomas Matthews, which passed in 1747, as part of the manor of Loughton, to the Whitaker Trustees, a part of which cottage still remains embedded in the subsequent extensions *[of the house at Ash Green today].* Of this cottage and land of some 3 roods and 35 perches, Charles Lane had a lease for a year from Anne Whitaker dated 29 July 1812, at a peppercorn rent and a release in fee on the next day. In February 1812 Thomas and Susannah Matthews sold a $1/4$ acre, late property of the vendor's father for 17 guineas, covenanting to make surrender or deed if necessary, this land said to be adjoining his premises. Mr Lane bought this land from Mr Hatherill in April 1812 for £30. This appears to be the far end of the garden *[the orchard]* opposite Sunnybank *[on Woodbury Hill]* but if so, between it and Mr Lane's other acquisition (Matthews' cottage) was interposed a cottage and garden, the history of which begins with a Court Roll of 1795, when Benjamin Bigg had a grant of 8 rods of waste, which would appear to have extended itself as time went on, to build a cottage.

In 1835 Mr Lane acquired this copyhold tenement of now 38 rods from Joseph Bigg for £100, and in 1836 he had a grant of the waste of 7 perches 22 yards to the south, that is in front of it, and between it and a detached plot, called the "circular garden", which Mr Lane seems to have acquired from Robert Grout in 1812, for the sum of thirty shillings.

In 1858 the Crown rights over the 7.22p (8 perches) were granted to Eliza Watson (*née* Lane). The waste is said to be north of Bigg's property, but the parish map of 1820 (circa) refutes this, showing it to the south east with the circular garden below it.

In addition to his purchases Mr Lane had grants of waste in 1812, in all 2 roods 17p enrolled (with plans) in the Court of Attachments (22 April 1824). More than half of this went to augment the Woolard-Matthews property, a small bit (4p 2yds) being near Bigg's cottage, the rest belonged to Sunnybank.

I am not quite sure, even now, that I have got it all quite straight, but I think that it is approximately so, and it only remains to add the 1r 28p awarded by the Arbitrator *[under the Epping Forest Act 1878]* by order dated 1881.'

In summary, today's house at Ash Green started as the Woolard/Matthews cottage, and the former gardener's cottage started as Bigg's cottage. Waller goes on to describe in more detail the house:

'Charles Lane seems to have paid a first visit to Loughton in 1804 and to have moved thither in 1807. (He rented property until 1813 by which time the alterations to Matthews' cottage were complete.) These it seems were made at both ends – a kitchen and closet, with what was known as the "bird room" over it and a back staircase. (Stuffed birds were in the cases now in the passage downstairs) and at the other end the rooms much as they are now, I suppose. But after the death of the Lanes, the Watsons made considerable alterations, though I do not think that they rebuilt that end entirely. The staircase was originally just inside the front door: the Watson's must have moved it round the corner, and we took it further still, to where it now is.

The garden was laid out at the same time, being previously more or less, as I gather, a wood. Grout, who afterwards kept the Gardeners' Arms, was gardener then and did a good deal of it. He lived to be very old, and his daughter, who kept the shop, died the other day, aged 50-60. The present gardener's cottage (Bigg's tenement) was at one time occupied by the curate of the parish. The paddock had iron hurdles round it, and the carriage horse used to be turned into it on days when we had no other exercise. *[Waller adds a note in pencil at the bottom of the page:* I began planting daffodils 20 years or more ago (1890) and have scattered seed yearly. *Local residents remember the annual show of daffodils in the orchard up until as recently as 1980.]*

The Grotto was made in Mr Lane's time – it was thatched and when I had the thatch off, thinking it to be in a very bad state, there was such a mass of straw that no rain could have got in for years and a little top-patching would have kept it going – However, it was too late. New thatch was estimated to cost £20-25. *[The Grotto no longer exists.]*'

In the topographical survey in his *Loughton in Essex,* Waller concludes the section on Ash Green by saying:

'The seven parcels of land being thus amalgamated, and the old bound-aries obliterated, neither lord nor tenant knew for certain what was free-hold and what was copyhold, and it was not until after the property had been enfranchised, that the present owner gradually accumulated the materials from which the present account is composed.'

Waller drew many plans showing all the field numbers around Ash Green and for the whole parish, based on various demesne surveys (1739) and Tithe Commutation Awards (1850). In the latter respect field numbers 454, 457, 458 and 459 form the main parcels of the land at Ash Green together with the adjoining areas of waste that were enclosed.

The Ordnance Survey map of 1872 incorrectly called the house at Ash Green, 'York House'. This annoyed Waller sufficiently for him to draw attention to the error in his will which contains a useful summary of all the land in Loughton that he owned.

During the time that William Waller lived at Ash Green he built a new wing to the house in 1885 and had the shield from his coat of arms placed in stonework on the outside of the chimney breast. In 1903 new stables were con-structed on the Baldwins Hill side of the garden and a boundary stone on the stable wall marks this event. The stone confuses some by referring to 'WCW-MW'. The 'MW' refers to his wife Emma, who was known as Minnie.

On the south western side of the old Queen Anne part of the house a large conservatory/greenhouse existed until 1979. This was well known for a very old vine which had extended itself throughout the conservatory.

The housing developments of the early 1980s saw many old features of the garden disappear. The pond and the remains of the gardener's cottage, together with the orchard, are now covered by the eleven houses of Waller's Hoppet. A magnificent aged Sweet Chestnut is no more. However, the remaining part of the garden is still very attractive with preservation orders on six old trees includ-ing yews, oaks, ash and a younger sweet chestnut.

OTHER LAND AND PROPERTY OWNED BY WALLER

Between 1880 and his death in 1917 Waller purchased the freeholds of various cottages in the parish and also built some houses on land that he had acquired. The result was that by 1917 Waller had accumulated a considerable amount of property. His will lists the property and beneficiaries as:

'I give:

1. The six cottages on York Hill Green (opposite the Gardeners' Arms) described in a Court Roll of 25 April 1715 as on the waste soil and held by Ann Bridge by a rent of two capons, which cottages having bought them of Mr Henry Lincoln in 1882 I enfranchised and enlarged, and

2. The detached cottage adjoining the said cottages long occupied by Mrs Eke and bought by me of Thomas Hatherill's executors, and

3. The house and land described in a Court Roll of 25 April 1715 as being on the waste soil and granted to Andrew Dawges long known as Sunnybank and by me inherited enfranchised and rebuilt, and

4. The freehold pightle or hoppet adjoining Sunnybank now into three parts divided whereof one part lies to the west within the holly hedge and forms a curtilage to Sunnybank and another lies east of the same holly hedge and a third has upon it a cottage by me recently erected now in the occupation of Mr Wyatt and known as Southbank all of which three were of old known as Enever's or Bright's land or Kent's Hoppet and by me inherited, and

5. The two semi-detached cottages known as White Thorn Cottages situate on Baldwins Hill recently by me erected on land purchased on the death of Samuel Wilks, and

6. The two semi-detached houses known as Eyres Croft and Slyders Gate by me recently built on part of the Uplands Estate and now in the occupation of Mr Hutchinson and Dr Culpin, to my son Ambrose.

And as to the land on Church Hill in Loughton recently purchased by me with the house erected thereon and known as Priests Garth, I give to my daughter Evelyn.'

Waller also owned some land opposite the entrance to Ash Green. This was called Forest Field but by the time that he made his will this had been divided, by the construction of St John's Road, into Forest Fields East and West. This land he left to his wife together with the main house and gardens at Ash Green.

The history of the principal houses referred to above is of some local interest, if only because the houses still exist today.

Sunnybank

This house, rebuilt by Waller in 1888-89 was on copyhold land which he enfranchised. In 1715 John Wroth granted the reversion of the land to Andrew Dawges on the death of his mother, as a tenement on the waste soil on King's Hill. After passing through several hands, as set out in the Court Rolls, it came to John Higgins, higler, who on 19 February 1814 made it over to Charles Lane for £210 – the area on the Tithe map is shown as 0a 3r 37p.

Adjacent to this copyhold was a small freehold, described in 1747 as 'that cottage with the land thereto belonging now or late in the tenure of John Johnson'. This land, on which a cottage formerly stood, passed from Anne Whitaker to Charles Lane on 30 July 1812, as Enever's alias Bright's land, alias Kent's Hoppet. This was let as a paddock, with Sunnybank, which in 1835 was let on seven years lease to Dr Southwood-Smith at £28 pa, tenant doing repairs.

Rents seem to have fallen, for in 1853 another tenant, from quarter to quarter, had it for £24 with two acres more or less. It was occupied at one time by the hymn writer Sarah Flower Adams. For a long time the house was occupied by Eaton, who formerly kept the King's Head Inn. On his death, Clement of the Phoenix Fire Office had it – his wife being in some sort a kinswoman of Eaton's, and it was during his tenancy, at £28, that the new house was built.

This attractive house still stands today – built in red brick, on Woodbury Hill, but it has been divided into two semi-detached houses. The shield from the Waller coat of arms is in stone on the front of the house with the date 1888.

Southbank

This house was also built by Waller in 1888. However, Waller considered it a costly investment: 'by reason of poor tenants and underpinning and drainage problems.' This is not surprising as the house stands on very steeply raked land. Vaughan Nash lived in it and was in 1911 Secretary to the Prime Minister. The house has recently (Spring 2000) been the subject of a planning application for demolition, to be replaced by two new houses. The application has

Above: Ash Green House at time of construction of new stables in 1903
Below: Eyres Croft and Slyders Gate on Church Hill in 1905, built by Waller in 1904

Above: Priests Garth in 1906 (built by Waller) and Arnill's Forge, on Church Hill
Below: On York Hill, October 1905

been rejected and further proposals are awaited. Southbank and Sunnybank were designed by James Cubitt, the architect.

Cottages on York Hill Green

The old wooden cottages opposite the Gardener's Arms at the north west end of the Green date back to 1715 when the lord of the manor granted to Ann Bridge a cottage and garden on the waste soil to be held by a rent of two capons at the will of the lord of the manor. From her the property passed through many hands, and in1838 the one copyhold cottage had become six – three brick and three wooden. In 1842 Chalkley Gould, farmer, bought them for £200. In 1847 Henry Lincoln paid £210 for them and a court fine of £43. He, having enfranchised at Waller's cost, for £195, sold the cottages to Waller in 1882 for £610, but as Waller comments:

'What with one thing and another, they cost me in the final event £1,192, repairs being £317. They have returned perhaps 3% and are a vanishing security. However, they kept the Hill [York] more or less rural.'

The adjoining detached cottage, Hatherill's, Waller bought later. He was unable to find out much about the origin of this cottage. Hatherill was a forest keeper. The cottage was occupied for many years by the Eke family, whose father and son were blacksmiths.

As a tailpiece Waller notes that opposite these cottages in the hedge of Ash Green, by the orchard, a pillar box exists (it is still there). His wife was at Ash Green (in about 1880) when the pillar box was put up and laid a brick at the bottom, not thinking how often her letters would be posted there (until her death in 1939).

Eyres Croft and Slyders Gate

Waller had these semi-detached houses built in 1904. The cast iron box at the head of the drainpipe still shows this date. Although Waller described them in 1911 as on the Uplands Estate, they are in fact on the east side of Church Hill, backing on to the Uplands. The houses names originate from a house built nearby in 1682 and called Slyders and the 14 acres that went with it and which were held by John and Sarah Eyre.

Alma Cottage

Although not referred to in his will, Waller for a time owned Alma Cottage in York Hill. It originated in an eight rod grant in 1795 by Anne Whitaker to a labourer at 2s 6d. Waller describes it as a small wooden box but in 1889 he paid £260 and fines on admission of £30 and the enfranchisement cost £80 – altogether the cottage cost him £435. In 1901 he sold it for £454 to Godfrey Lomer, who drove a road (now Steeds Way) from the cottage up to Loughton Lodge where he was to later live and built in Alma Cottage's garden two large semi-detached houses. On his death he left an estate of £60,000, a fortune at that time. The cottage's name came from the Battle of Alma in 1854 but why it was called this and what it was called before then are not known.

It has already been seen that William Waller inherited Ash Green and other property from his aunt, Jane Miller Waller, who in turn had inherited from Eliza Watson, the daughter of Charles Lane. However, it is clear that Waller exercised a degree of business acumen in purchasing further land and building houses. He sold the freehold of some of the properties during his lifetime but others were left to be sold later by his family.

Alma Cottage, York Hill in 1905 (Waller owned the cottage for a short while)

Above: Waltham Abbey
Below: W C Waller's sons outside Ash Green (c 1903)

Plate 1   W C Waller's Coat of Arms granted in 1887

Plate 2   Jane Miller Waller (1800-1881)
(Portrait by Edward Hughes 1881)

Plate 3 Drawing by Eliza Watson of *view from Ash Green towards High Beach* (c 1850)

III

Plate 4 Ash Green House today

Plate 5 Ash Green House today, rear garden

Plate 6 Sunnybank, Woodbury Hill, today, built by Waller in 1888

Plate 7 Sunnybank, Woodbury Hill, today, showing Waller 'Arms'

Plate 8 York Hill Green cottages today (Waller bought the freehold in 1882)

Plate 9 St John's Church, Loughton: lych gate, a memorial to Vera Waller

Plate 10 St John's Church, Loughton: window and brass memorials to W C Waller and his son Geoffrey

Plate 11 Cottages at Woodbury Hole (Hollow)

XI

Plate 12 Whitaker's Almshouses, Arewater Green

Plate 13   Hornbeams in Epping Forest

Plate 14 Beeches in Epping Forest

Golding's Hill, Loughton.

Plate 15 Goldings Hill, Loughton, in about 1900

Plate 16 Cottage at York Hill Green, Loughton, June 2000

XVI

3
LOUGHTON IN ESSEX

By 1889 William Waller had been living in Loughton for over fifteen years. During this time he was completing his education at Oxford and was commencing his studies at the Inner Temple. He and his wife Minnie had started a family and the house at Ash Green had been extended. Their circle of friends was no doubt widening with the Pellys, the Dents and the Minets prominent.

Like many Victorians, attendance at and participation in the affairs of the local church almost went without saying, and the more well known members of the church had their own pews, as was the case with Waller at St John's in Loughton.

THE PARISH MAGAZINE

We have already seen that as early as 1871 Waller had been awarded a prize at King's College for Modern History, and it may not be altogether surprising to find him in 1889 starting to contribute to the Loughton Parish Magazine short notes (or at least he called them short) on parochial history. These were followed by some extracts of early wills from notes he made in the Principal Probate Registry.

Waller decided that it was worth trying to produce a narrative for a whole series of articles which were to appear in the Parish Magazine over a period of eleven years from 1889 to 1900. The result was a volume containing in all some 230 pages. Waller arranged with the printer of the Parish Magazine, A B Davis of Epping, that an extra twelve copies of each monthly instalment were pulled off, on large paper. On completion of the series these were bound in stiff board covers under the title *Loughton in Essex.*

Waller gave copies to his friends: J C Challenor-Smith, W Minet and the Rev. J Whitaker Maitland. Another six copies were given to the following institutions: the British Museum, Guildhall Library (City of London), Cambridge University Library, Bodleian Library (Oxford), Society of Antiquaries and Harvard College USA. Waller kept his own 'master' copy on which he subsequently made annotations. Another copy was bound in morocco in two volumes and contained many photographs, and the final copy of the twelve was described as imperfect. Each copy was numbered with a short manuscript note written by the author to the recipient hoping that they would accept the book.

THE HISTORY OF THE MANOR AND PARISH

Waller entitled the first part of the book: 'collections illustrative of the history of the manor and parish'. A frontispiece showed a rough plan of the parish of Loughton, drawn by Waller, based on the demesne survey of 1739 with the field names and numbers of that time and the corresponding numbers based on the Ordnance Survey of 1872. The original of this map is in the Waller archive at the Essex Record Office.

Waller introduces the ancient history of Loughton by quoting the relevant extract from Morant's *History of Essex and its Antiquities,* published in 1768, in which he records that the name of this parish is written in five different ways apart from the current usage: Lochintun, Lockton, Loketon, Lucton and Lukentone. He suggests that it is derived from the Saxon words 'loc', an inclosure, and 'tun', a town or village.

In commencing his own narrative, Waller points out that Loughton, Essex, is by no means the only place of the name in England. Loughton Magna and Loughton Parva occur in Buckinghamshire, Loughton in the Forest of Clee is in Shropshire, Loughton near Folkingham is in Lincolnshire, with the alternative forms of Lowton in Lancashire, Lucton in Herefordshire and Lockton in Yorkshire.

Edward the Confessor and Domesday

The earliest mention of Loughton in Essex is perhaps to be found in a Charter of Edward the Confessor, dated 1062. Here it is written as Lukinton. About a quarter of a century later it is written in Domesday Book as Lochetuna and Lochintuna. During the thirteenth and fourteenth centuries Luketon is perhaps the commonest form and it is not until the sixteenth century that the form Loughton seems to have come into common use.

Your most obedient humble Servant

Phil. Morant

Philip Morant – Essex Historian

Lukinton or Lochetuna did not embrace the whole area of what is now included within the parish of Loughton. We have to search among the seventeen manors with which Earl Harold endowed his monastery of the Holy Cross at Waltham, to find two manors which adjoined Lukinton. The manors of Tippedene and Alwartun or Alwertuna are identified as those of Debden and Alderton of today. Waller goes into much detail explaining the possible derivations of each name and their usage in various MSS from the time of the first Charter of Edward the Confessor.

He also calculated that, if a 'hide', as a measure of land, is taken as 120 acres, then the eight estates referred to in the Domesday survey, covered no less than 2,165 acres. In 1850 the area of land in private ownership in Loughton, exclusive of the Forest, water and roads, amounted to 2,558 acres, the conclusion being that rather less than 400 acres were taken from the Forest during the many hundred years which elapsed between the Conquest and the Tithe Commutation Award. Waller's comment was very relevant bearing in mind that he was writing shortly after Epping Forest had been saved from the illegal enclosures in the earlier part of the nineteenth century.

A description of the tenants of each of the estates follows and quotes the obligations to the lord of the manor of two tenants: Robert Terry and William Ram. Both had to work for the lord twice in every week, but the occurrence of a festival, except at Christmas, Easter and Whitsuntide, made no difference to Terry whereas Ram was quit a half day's work. Waller adds a word or two as to the conditions of life in which the tenants and their workers lived. The houses of the tenants, with their gardens and pightles or hoppets, were probably clustered together in three separate villages, the sites of which can now hardly be guessed at. The holdings consisted, not of compact little farms lying as it were in a ring fence, but a number of acre or half acre strips scattered all over the common fields.

The fourteenth century

We now move forward to the fourteenth century where historical researches are mainly confined to the contributions the village made to the taxation of the realm. The Forest Rolls, however, furnish a few incidental items of interest. In the taxation records we see for the first time the names of Loughton families which are to occur for several centuries thereafter, even if they are today only known as the names of roads in the district. In returns for 1320 and 1327 we see included John Traps (Trapps Hill), John Goldyng (Goldings Hill), Geoffrey Algor (Algers Road) and John de Hatfield (Hatfields).

Few of the early records of the Forest Courts have been preserved but Waller managed to find some. He quotes offences against the King's deer, including in 1276 two deer having been taken in Depedene Wood, in Waltham Forest and carried off to London without warrant. The offence had occurred six years earlier but the offenders were only brought to justice much later owing to the complicated machinery of the Forest Courts. Next we find offences against the 'vert'. Godfrey Bigge and Robert, son of Stephen the Miller, were each fined 12d for cutting vert in Loughton Forest. (Could Bigge be from the same family that was to live in the cottage on what became the orchard at Ash Green?)

Even in the fourteenth century we find local inhabitants enclosing the forest waste. In 1333 a charge is brought against Theobald de Loketon for enclosing a piece of land two perches long and one perch wide, which lay before his gate, and was on the soil of the Abbot of Waltham.

In the survey of 1739, what we today call Warren Hill on which is the residence of the Superintendent of Epping Forest, was shown as Mill Hill. The Mill had ceased to exist by then but a century earlier, in 1650 John Wignall and Robert Dawges were presented at the Loughton Manor Court for cutting down a great oak tree there, worth ten shillings.

Waller regrets that for many years manorial rolls have been sold by the cartload and boiled down into size and gelatine, yet they contain material of priceless value to the historian. He therefore thinks it worthwhile to translate the greater part of two early rolls for 1403-04. They reveal Loughton as a small community practically autonomous and self-sufficient. For the prevention and detection of crime and misdemeanour there was the tithing, in which every male above the age of twelve years was bound by statute to be enrolled. Nuisances were abated and ruinous tenements put into habitable repair without the aid of an authority sitting at Epping or Whitehall (Westminster). Local ale-conners held the place of public analysts and inspectors of weights and measures. Forest trespasses were punished without recourse to the Bench.

Lands and houses were transferred from hand to hand with brief formalities and adequate publicity, the rolls of the Court serving as a register. Cases of assault and battery, which fell under the law of trespass, were settled without a journey to Waltham, as also were actions for breach of contract. Thefts, too, came within the remit of the local Court.

The sixteenth century

The opening of the sixteenth century saw the Tudor dynasty firmly established on the throne. Henry VII died in April 1509, and Henry VIII, a lad of eighteen, succeeded to his hoarded millions and his throne. It is probable that the good people of Loughton little dreamed that the handsome, generous Prince, who often came hunting in their forest, was fated to leave behind him the record of a reign, rapacious, blood stained, pitiless, or so Waller thought!

In 1522 the Abbot and Canons of the Holy Cross at Waltham granted a long lease of their manor of Loughton to John Stoner. Waller reprints the terms of the full lease. In 1535 George Stoner, son and heir of John Stoner of Loughton is granted a further lease of forty years. The terms of the new lease are similar to the first one, and include the obligations to keep repaired all buildings and to keep clean the river (Roding). In leasing out his manors and farms, the Abbot doubtless came twice a year to hold the Manor Courts. The Court held in April 1539 dealt with all manner of elections and offences and these are reprinted in full by Waller.

On 23 March 1540 there was signed at the Chapter House the deed by which the Abbot and Canons made over their possessions to the King. The Abbey lands now passed into the management of the newly erected 'Court of the Augmentations of the Revenues of the Crown'. The detailed accounts for the next fiscal year in respect of Loughton show the grand total of £9 5s 5d, collected by John Highame, the bailiff and collector of rents.

Under the reign of Edward VI a temporary change took place. On 4 April 1551 Edward granted the manor and advowson, with other lands elsewhere, to Sir Thomas Darcy, to hold by the service of one Knight's fee and certain small payments yearly to the Court of Augmentations, including one of 15s 6d in respect of the manor of Loughton. However, Darcy kept the manor for little more than a year when he exchanged it with the King for an estate in Surrey. A further change took place in May 1553 when Loughton became the property of the King's sister, Princess Mary. Again this is short lived as we find that in the next year the accounts record the incorporation of the manor into the Duchy of Lancaster.

Waller found in the Public Record Office the records of two courts held in Loughton in Queen Elizabeth's time. He gives the substance of these courts held in 1585 and 1593.

The seventeenth and eighteenth centuries

With the seventeenth and eighteenth centuries we enter a period when the material for the history of Loughton becomes more abundant and consequently less easy to review in this memoir. As we will see later from Waller's contributions to the Essex Archaeological Society and the Essex Field Club, he spent much time researching the history of the Stoner/Stonard and Wroth families who occupied Loughton Hall and were Lords of the Manor during this period.

A survey of the manor in 1612, together with an earlier survey in 1608 of the timber in the manor, provide a useful guide as to the area of forest, arable land and pasture. A survey in 1739 showed a total area of 1,319 acres. Some seven years after the survey was made, Lord Rochford sold the manor to William Whitaker, Alderman of London. On his death in 1752 it passed to Anne, his second wife, who in 1770 was succeeded by her daughter, also named Anne. She, dying unmarried in 1825, devised her estate to John Maitland of Woodford Hall, the grandfather of John Whitaker Maitland who was Lord of the Manor at the time Waller was writing his history of Loughton.

It had taken Waller four years to complete thus far his history of Loughton. For the history of the nineteenth century we have to look in the Minute Books of the Loughton Vestry and Waller's perambulations of Loughton which are included in the appendices to his book, and other sections of this memoir. The above notes barely do justice to the amount of detailed information which was included initially in the monthly instalments of the Parish Magazine. Waller had made searches at the British Museum, the Public Record Office and elsewhere in Essex to prepare his articles. The history had been recited in a roughly chronological order. He now turned to describe some specific aspects in further detail which he did by adding a number of appendices to his book.

Court Rolls

Waller's frequent visits to the Public Record Office had brought to light the existence of some early Court Rolls which had not previously been studied. In the first part of his history of Loughton he had quoted from these Rolls but in the appendices he goes into further detail.

Essex Assize Rolls

As in the case of the Manor Court Rolls, so in that of the rolls of the Courts of the King's Justices Itinerant, the historian is able to find what material there is relating to a particular county. The earliest existing Assize Roll for Essex is dated Chelmsford, 28 October 1226, but Loughton only appears in it once, and then merely as giving a name to the defendant in a case of warranty.

Loughton itself first appears in 1234 in relation to a charge of sheep stealing and other robberies. In or before 1248 Martin Shepherd of Harle, slew Geoffrey, son of Stephen de Lukenton in Luketon Wood. He was afterwards taken, imprisoned at Colchester and subsequently convicted and hanged. In 1317 Godfrey le Hauk was charged with breaking and entering into the house of Matilda Bigge and stealthily carrying off cloths, fur and woollen yarn and a sheaf of wheat. But, in spite of all, he went free. There follow many other examples of the criminal and legal history of Loughton mainly in the thirteenth and fourteenth centuries, several of which bear similarities to today.

Additional Lay Subsidy Rolls

The main purpose of these rolls to the historian was in estimating pretty closely the population of towns and villages. The first general Hearth, or Chimney, Tax was imposed by Charles II in 1662. Waller quotes a roll dated 1666 which gave the number of all and singular the hearths and stoves in Loughton with the names of the persons and the number of hearths in their homes. A later list dated 24 November 1707 shows the contributions to the Poor Rate made in Loughton.

The Rectors of Loughton

With his active participation in the affairs of St John's Church in Loughton, it is no surprise to find that Waller did some research into the Rectors of Loughton. His principal source was Newcourt's *Repertorium: the Ecclesiastical Parochial History of the Diocese of London,* published in 1708-10. However, he was able to add other names from his researches. More recent histories of St Nicholas and St John's churches in Loughton have been written by Percy Thompson and others, but Waller's commentary on the Rectors (up to 1900) remains a definitive work.

The Progress of Instruction in Loughton

This is a short note on education in Loughton and the involvement of the Church and charities. Waller came across some sundry school accounts and gives details of donations to, and the cost of maintaining the School at Loughton in the eighteenth and early nineteenth centuries.

The Minutes of the Loughton Vestry 1844-1869

This Minute Book of the Vestry covers the twenty-five years before Jane Miller Waller came to live in Loughton with Eliza Watson. William Waller was to play a prominent part in the Vestry from shortly after he arrived in Loughton until his death. Another Minute Book of the Vestry for the period 1869-1908 is in the Waller archive at the Essex Record Office.

When St John's Church was built in 1845 a Church rate produced £1,000, to which so far as the Minutes of 1846 show, no opposition was made. But by 1855 a murmur of discontent to high Church rates was becoming audible.

A large space in the Minutes is taken up by statements as to the Potato (allotment) Grounds: changes to the occupancies, prize awards and incidental matters. In 1859 a resolution included a condition that if any tenants were found working on Sundays, they shall forfeit their ground in consequence.

References to emigration occur on two occasions. In March 1852 it was agreed that £2 per head be given to any person wishing to emigrate.

The Minutes of the Vestry are in large measure taken up with the matters of local taxation and assessments. Until the East London (Water) Company's mains were laid, water was at times a scarce commodity in Loughton, and the fact is emphasised by pumps being regarded as a source of wealth separately rateable. The development and repair of roads also regularly occupied the Vestry.

What today is called King's Green, which is now the site of Loughton's memorial to the dead of two World Wars, was previously known as Cage Green, as it contained a small lock-up. This was removed in 1865.

With the growth of the village, difficulties as to its sanitary condition arose. In 1848 a Committee was formed to try to improve matters. However, there was an outbreak of smallpox in 1852. In 1865 it was resolved to form a main sewer to carry off the sewage from the Smart's Lane district.

Genealogical and Topographical

This is the longest but the most interesting of the appendices, as it contains a perambulation of Loughton Parish by Waller in which he comments on the history of various fields and buildings and some of the local people. Waller was to add to this in his *An Itinerary of Loughton*, which was written between 1905 and 1912, and in which more is said about the people then living in Loughton as his contemporaries. It will be sufficient here to cite one or two examples from the genealogical and topographical survey and to leave the main commentary to his later Itinerary in the next section of this memoir.

North's Farm was a freehold in which were included the two ancient copyholds of Edwards or Eddowes and Baalands. From 1619 to 1682 they were in separate ownership. A John North was the occupier in 1717 and 1792 and is likely to be the man from whom the farm got its name. Abutting on to North's Farm and extending to beyond Albion Hill was the estate which down to 1854 belonged to the Powell family.

Opposite the foot of Albion Hill was the Bull's Head, which was an ale-house with six adjacent cottages, long known as the Barrack. The Bull's Head and cottages are

Above: Ashfield Lodge, Baldwins Hill in 1885 (demolished in 1960)
Below: Clay Hills, Trapps Hill, in 1903

Above: Ray (Ree) House, Englands Lane in 1904, (demolished in 1906)
Below: 'New Lodge' and the "Fairmead Oak' in about 1890, now demolished

gone and in their place Augusta Villas were built in the 1890s. Another ale-house which no longer exists was the White Lyon, at the other end of the village on Goldings Hill. In 1743 it appears in the ownership of Richard Clay under the following description: the tenement now known by the name or sign of the White Lyon on Goldings Hill, with three roods of pasture, now in the occupation of Richard Gentry. In 1777 Richard Lomas Clay, the son, had license to pull the ale-house down.

On the western side of Goldings Hill lay a large block described as Poor's Piece Potato Ground, containing over two acres. The history of this appears in the rolls for May 1813, when Miss Whitaker granted to the Rector of Loughton a parcel of waste between the Poor House, on Baldwins Hill, and the High Road. The Rector and his successors were to hold the land for the use and benefit of such of the poor and industrious inhabitants of the Parish as the Rector may nominate. A further grant of three acres brought the Allotment to its present size.

Behind the Allotment Ground there existed a cluster of sixteen very small enclosures making up nearly three acres, mainly consisting of gardens but including a few cottages. In one of these cottages lived George Baldwin, but following his death it was used for the poor of the parish. Shortly after Miss Whitaker died in 1825, leaving in her will £1,000 towards the improvement of the Poor House, the trustees decided to build anew and in 1826 John Maitland made a grant of waste on which the Whitaker Almshouses now stand at Arewater Green. Jane Miller Waller was to leave a small bequest to the residents of the Almshouses and this charity continues today, with William Waller's granddaughter visiting the Almshouses every six months to distribute the benefit.

It was not until 1865 that Baldwins Hill from Ashfield Lodge to Goldings Hill became a metalled road, having been until then a track in the forest.

Waller continues his perambulation describing the White House estate which lay between Ashfields and Pump Hill, and through which St John's Road was later constructed. Next we come to Ash Green, Waller's home, and the other property that he owned in the cluster of buildings around the top of York Hill and Woodbury Hill, much of which had been previously owned by Charles Lane and the Watsons.

The Habgood estate between Staples Road, Forest Road and the High Road derives its name from James Habgood of Fish Street Hill, London, a haberdasher. Under his will of 1849, his son inherited a cottage with ponds and out-buildings and which subsequently became the granaries and offices of Messrs Gould and Sons, and which were demolished twenty years ago to be replaced by a super-market.

Waller continues south along the High Road noting that Smart's Lane was once known as Allards Lane and that Allards Grove should properly be called Collards Grove, now in fact named Ollards Grove.

Waller explains the history of the area surrounding Loughton Hall and Rectory Lane, one of the first-settled parts of Loughton, but with few old buildings left and only the old field names used as street names to remind us of its early history. He has little to say about the land lying to the east of the High Road from Trapps Hill to Algers Road, as in his time this was mainly farmland on which he had already commented in the main part of his book. The railway was the only major development in his time in this part of Loughton and it was not until the twentieth century that Alderton Hill and Spareleaze Hill were developed.

Loughton 150 Years Ago

This consists of an article which appeared in the Parish Magazine in 1890 and was based on the records of the Vestries held between the years 1720 and 1741. It gives a glimpse of by-gone village life and customs in days when the population was but sparse, and the council of elders, in Parish Vestry assembled, bore still some resemblance to a family gathering at which no strange face was seen.

Charters and Extents

Waller reprints here translations of extracts from some ancient Charters which he had used in his research. The main source was Harleian MS 4809.

TRANSCRIPTS AND ABSTRACTS OF SOME OLD WILLS RELATING TO LOUGHTON

Part II of *Loughton in Essex* consists of extracts from some seventy wills of former Loughton residents. The Wroths and the Stonards figure prominently but other less well known persons are also included.

Waller also provides an invaluable index for each of the two parts of his book.

LOUGHTON IN ESSEX.

PART I.

COLLECTIONS ILLUSTRATIVE OF THE HISTORY OF THE MANOR AND PARISH, WITH INDEX.

PART II.

TRANSCRIPTS AND ABSTRACTS OF SOME OLD WILLS RELATING TO LOUGHTON, WITH INDEX.

BY

WILLIAM CHAPMAN WALLER, M.A., F.S.A.
OF THE INNER TEMPLE, BARRISTER-AT-LAW.

EPPING: ALFRED B. DAVIS,
1889-1900

Title page from *Loughton in Essex*

MISCELLANEOUS NOTES

Between 1890 and 1916 Waller made some notes under the title 'Odds and Ends' and which also included a number of newspaper cuttings of the time. The notes were in part used for the genealogical and topographical survey in *Loughton in Essex*. However, they contain a number of items of interest which are not in the book or in Waller's *An Itinerary of Loughton*. Each note is dated but the entries are random and in manuscript form. The following extracts are taken from volume I which covered the period 1890-95.

11 October 1890
'Highwaymen'. James Wilks, the road surveyor (a man over seventy as I judge) tells me that he remembers when most of the houses had what he called a 'Turpin-trap', ie a flap door shutting down over the head of the staircase – this was let down when all had gone upstairs and a stick fixed on it and against the ceiling above to keep it from being opened from beneath.

'Deer-stealing'. James Wilks also told me that in winter time, on a farm which stood near where Paul's Nursery now is and the house called 'The Dragons', they used to entice the deer in and pick out the best, which never went out again. (The man on Goldings Hill, according to Mr Allen, used to poach also and the pond was full of horns and bones.)

6 August 1892
Drove over and called on Mrs Powell at Buckhurst Hill. Showed her my sketch of old Loughton Hall – which she said was fairly as she remembered it. It was burnt down on Xmas Eve [in fact two weeks earlier] – she saw the flames from her windows (at Beech now Nuneham House) at six in the morning and when she went to the afternoon service (there was none in the morning, for fear of fire) the house was a shell. There was no water to be had – snow was on the ground and all was frozen.

April 1893
A propos of my notes on old Loughton Hall in the E.N. *(Essex Naturalist),* Mr Maitland told me that the Library was the collection of Miss Whitaker, his grandfather, and (I think) Dr Bliss. Inter alia a copy of Magna Carta in gold letters, and the petition to Queen Elizabeth by inhabitants of Loughton against having the road made – (I have been told also the reason alleged was that the vices of London would be brought down) were lost in the fire.

April 1894
A propos of the voluminous correspondence anent Epping Forest, the Essex Field Club on Saturday met at Theydon and went through the

Forest. I had been up at Gaynes Park Hall, where C.M. *[Chisenhale Marsh]* had come on the papers missing from those calendared in the 'His. MS Com Rep.' *[Historical Manuscripts Commission Report]* and I joined the cavalcade at three. One hundred to one hundred and fifty people there. The meeting ended with 'tea and talk' at the Royal Forest Hotel – but I couldn't go. Monk Wood, it seems was divided up into ten parts, one of which was formerly cut each year – so said E N Buxton, on Rector's authority. Personally I do not think the thinning overdone.

December 1894
The First Parish Meeting under the new Act was held in the Lopping Hall on Tuesday, 4 December, at 7pm. The great hall was by no means full, but there was a very good attendance of ratepayers. Mr Vincent, the master of a private school, was voted to the chair; Mr Tee and Mr Robin Allen (who withdrew) being the only others proposed. He received nominations – (Lawford pencilled one for Vicar Allen and I seconded it, in the room) – 33 in number – later he read them out, and said no one could withdraw except by writing to the Returning officer. This was corrected owing to Tee's calling attention to some section or other: but no one did withdraw.

The Chairman then ruled that each candidate could express his views. G P Claille, Board Schoolmaster, moved a limit of three minutes to each speech – and so we got through by 9 or 9.30. The meeting was extremely orderly and good tempered.

26 May 1895
The little square patch in the Forest not far from Earl's Path pond, but on the opposite side of the road and down the narrow green drive, was an enclosure. Some people named Anderson lived there in a van and cultivated the ground. It belonged to Chilton. The trees at the time of the enclosure were sold at a shilling a load – or stack – 'but there never was a stack because people carried them off as they cut'. This came out at a Labour Aid meeting, in response to my enquiry as to how the clearing came to be made at the back of Loughton Camp, where birches and oaks now grow. 'Durling' cleared it, and other patches, in the Forest. A clearing was made near Wake Valley ponds.

There are many other fascinating notes about Loughton in the 1890s, covering more than thirty pages of Waller's notebook. A further six volumes cover in a similar vein the next twenty years.

How can we assess the value of Waller's work? First, no other history of Loughton goes into as much detail. Secondly, we must be impressed by Waller's depth of sources for his research, some of it must have been laborious and painstaking but even if we accept the apology in his own Preface for the 'form or rather

formlessness of my book', the journey was well worthwhile.

At least seven of the original twelve bound copies still
exist. I have traced all the copies given to the institutions,
excepting only Harvard College. In addition, Waller's own
copy is now lodged with the British Library. The British
Library's other copy (donated to the British Museum) is
unique in that it contains seventeen photographs of
Loughton and its people at the end of the nineteenth century. Copy No 12, described as imperfect, is held at the
Essex Record Office. The odd copy was made up from
copies of the actual Parish Magazine and these may be
found in one or two libraries or are personally owned.
Perhaps this memoir will unearth other of the remaining
bound copies.

In 1903 Waller read a paper at a meeting of the Club
Literary Society in Loughton, which he subsequently had
reprinted on two occasions. This was a very abridged ver-
sion of some twenty pages, of his main work. It was titled
Loughton, Essex: a brief account of the Manor and Parish.
Copies are still to be found in libraries.

Golden's (Goldings) Hill in 1891

4
An Itinerary of Loughton

'An Itinerary of Loughton in the County of Essex
begun this fourth day of February 1905, by me,
William Chapman Waller, a resident there.'

With the above introduction Waller began what was to be one of his most fascinating works, as it combines his usual detailed historical research with a less academic commentary on the inhabitants of Loughton, all written in an almost conversational style. It was a work which he pursued intermittently over seven years with a last contribution in 1912. It seems likely that he intended to finish at this point as he had covered most parts of the village and its people with whom he was familiar.

In some ways it was surprising that he set out on this road, as his main work *Loughton in Essex*, had covered much of the ground. However, I think that there are two reasons for the Itinerary. First, Waller was able to refer to his earlier work and to update and expand parts. Secondly, as Waller said himself, it was a way of thanking historians of previous centuries, by writing a contemporary diary which some future historian might find of interest.

The document, of some eighty pages, is only in manuscript form in a notebook, but it is hoped to have it transcribed and published by the Loughton & District Historical Society. The original MS is in the possession of the Waller family. This memoir will therefore only dip into some of the more interesting items, which may also amplify or clarify comments on Waller's main history of Loughton.

By 1905 Waller had lived in Loughton for more than thirty years and he comments that there have been many changes. In the 1870s people went regularly to church and generally twice on Sunday. Now, he says, the occupants of the bigger houses are very irregular. Then one knew most people, at any rate by sight.

THE WAKE ARMS, GOLDINGS HILL, DEBDEN GREEN, LOUGHTON HALL AND HATFIELDS

Waller starts his Itinerary at the Wake Arms. Little was he to know the changes which were to happen to that Inn in the last twenty-five years of the twentieth century. He regrets that not many years ago one could see right across the Forest, which was pollarded until 1870 or so, to Abridge. Now the trees are of good size and the distant view is cut off. Waller proceeds down Goldings Hill and notes the Forest Keepers' Lodges just above Broadstrood, and passes Goldings Hill House, no longer there. For some time it was called the Manor House because the Maitlands lived there for a while, after the fire at Loughton Hall.

Further down the Hill, Waller passes the house which was later to be occupied by the author W W Jacobs (now recognised by a blue plaque). At the bottom of the Hill we turn left into Englands Lane where, even in Waller's time, most of the old cottages had been replaced, and on to Debden Green. Debden Hall in which 'Squire Williams' lived comes next. Waller knew him and describes him as a quaint old man, who stuck to the fashions of his younger days. He had been on the Stock Exchange and retired with a considerable fortune. At first a sister or two lived with him, but in Waller's time he was on his own. When Williams died there was a sale and Waller bought a few old books. He left little money but his Estate fetched £30-40,000. Debden Hall was bought by Mr Palmer, a printing ink manufacturer, who pulled it down and built anew.

Returning by way of Pyrles Lane we reach the old Rectory, which since Maitland rebuilt Loughton Hall, had constantly been let. On the other side of the road was Hatfields, occupied in 1909 by Frank Dent, a Churchwarden at St John's, and a close friend of Waller's. Dent had married Edward North Buxton's daughter Geraldine. Dent's children knew the Waller children and the boys in the families were at Marlborough School at the same time.

A brief mention is made of Loughton Hall in which John Whitaker Maitland was living but who was to die in 1910. Waller notes that Maitland's son Peregrine has always had some hip disease and uses walking sticks. 'It seems a sad thing and he seems an amiable lad.'

ALDERTON HILL, TRAPPS HILL
AND THE UPLANDS

Waller finds some new houses near Alderton Hall and is attracted by some of them. He mentions the names of two well known local architects: Egan and Tooley, who were involved, and recommends the latter to his friend Pelly who lived at Shortacres on the corner of Church Hill and St John's Road. In Trapps Hill two houses are noted as having been the residences of members of the Gould family. Egan was the architect of the house Brooklyn, demolished in about 1966, at the bottom of Trapps Hill.

Waller briefly returns towards Goldings Hill to mention the Uplands Estate and discusses at length the pedigree of the Rohrweger family. He refers to the semi-detached houses that he had built in 1904, called Eyres Croft and Slyders Gate. The forge, further up Church Hill was an ancient feature, demolished only in 1996.

A house called Meads is reached shortly before Church Lane. This ancient Loughton copyhold, together with Waller's house at Ash Green and one other on Church Hill, are now Grade II listed buildings.

It is February 1911 before Waller returns to his tour. He notes that some things have changed. John Whitaker Maitland has died and the new Rector is living in a small house on the Uplands Estate. This was the Rev Arthur Montford, about whom we are to hear more later (see Consistory Courts).

Waller has now crossed Church Hill and after referring to the Pellys at Shortacres he comes to what was one of Loughton's oldest houses, the White House, alas no more. His friend Peter Gellatly, the local solicitor and a Verderer, had moved from High Standing on Albion Hill to the White House and made great improvements and alterations to the house, but the house was to soon change hands again.

THE WOODBURYS

Waller moves on to Baldwins Hill and Ash Green about which we have heard much in an earlier section of this memoir. Passing through York Hill Green and along Woodbury Hill we come to the top of King's Hill and find the two Woodberries and mention of Robin Allen and his wife. Allen had been Secretary to Trinity House. Waller describes him as a cultured man with artistic talents. He mentions that years ago he used to help one of Allen's sons with his Latin and French, presumably as a schoolboy.

Woodbury Knoll, a large house on Woodbury Hill, overlooking the Forest, was built on the site of some old cottages. Next we come to 'The Hole', or as it is known today, 'Woodbury Hollow', still one of the most picturesque parts of Loughton. There are two old wooden boarded cottages and a more recent one built by the Zimmermans, who were prosperous toy merchants in London.

Loughton Lodge, if lacking in architectural distinction, has been occupied by two or three well known Loughton families, including the Lomers and the Chaters. An earlier building on this site was reputed to have been the temporary home in 1810 of Mary Ann Clarke, the mistress of the Duke of York, who was involved in a scandal of selling Army commissions at the beginning of the nineteenth century.

CHURCH HILL

Waller descended King's Hill and York Hill and arrived at the King's Head, which had been rebuilt recently in about 1906, but apparently was not doing good business. However, the butcher's shop next door was doing well and was run by Bosworth, a man of substance and a sportsman. Waller heads north again, up Church Hill and down towards the junction with Rectory Lane and Englands Lane. He mentions two ale-houses, the Bag o' Nails and the Plume of Feathers, the latter of which survives.

ST MARY'S PARISH

Waller is now writing in 1912 and, having exhausted St John's Parish, which he knew best, he crosses into St Mary's. The boundary is in the middle of the roads York Hill, the High Road and Trapps Hill. Moving along the High Road, Waller stops at a house known as the Shrubbery, which existed until the 1960s. In Waller's time this house was the abode of Dr Butler Harris, who came to Loughton and put up a plate and gradually got a practice.

Waller comments that he is great on germs and was, I think, the first to treat diphtheria by the new methods. He is great on motor cars, and built up his own electric light engine. However, there is prejudice against the Doctor by some people and Waller includes himself in this.

The Misses Barton, who kept the Post Office in the High Road, are described as very grumpy people, in succession to their father, also a grumpy person. The Post Office then lay in the angle between the High Road and Forest Road.

The former Baptist Chapel, now the Loughton Union Church, on the High Road between Ollards Grove and Upper Park, creates some interest for Waller. Cubitt was the architect of the Chapel, whom Waller described as a queer, mouse-like, little man, with white hair and a wonderful complexion. It was alleged that he never went to bed before three or four and got up at noon. However, he was an architect of some reputation and designed Sunnybank and Southbank for Waller.

Further along the road towards Buckhurst Hill we find a mixture of large houses and cottages. The former have been replaced by blocks of flats, such as Grange Court, and smaller housing developments such as Nafferton Close, both using the name of the old houses on the site. We arrive at Warren Hill, at the top of which lies the Warren House. We can end our journey by quoting from the last page of Waller's diary, writing as he was in 1912:

'The Superintendent of Epping Forest, living at the Warren, is F F McKenzie, who succeeded his father, and married a wife with pretty white hair, a kindly disposition and a good deal of money, a daughter of a Mrs Reed who lives at Chigwell Row and who takes about with her a bantam cock, as other people do a dog. It has been seen in Oxford Circus and was at a garden party at the Hamilton's – quite absurd.'

Even historians can be light-hearted at times, albeit with a note of disapproval.

Above: Alderton Hall in 1903
Below: The Old Rectory at Loughton (demolished in c 1960)

5
THE ESSEX FIELD CLUB

In the second half of the nineteenth century there was an increasing interest by local people in the natural history of their surroundings and county. This interest was widespread and included many of the better off inhabitants from various professions, as well as those qualified in botany, zoology and the other natural sciences of flora and fauna.

This led to the formation in January 1880 of the Epping Forest and County of Essex Naturalists' Field Club. The objects of the Club were the study and investigation of natural history, geology and prehistoric archaeology, of the county of Essex, the formation of a library of local scientific works, the formation of a museum and to promote a reverence for the natural features of the county.

Epping Forest had recently been saved by an Act of Parliament and the Corporation of London, and its 6,000 acres (after the Arbitrator has issued his final report) provided the perfect location for investigations into natural history. The two principal provisions of the Epping Forest Act of 1878 were that it should be an open space for the recreation and enjoyment of all people, and that the Conservators should wherever possible preserve the natural aspect.

Notwithstanding the close relationship with Epping Forest, it had been made clear by the President of the Field Club in his inaugural address, that the interests of the Club extended to the whole of Essex and by 1882 it had been decided that the name of the Club be simply the Essex Field Club and the report of its transactions to appear under the name of the *Essex Naturalist.*

Living in a Forest parish and knowing many of the local residents who had become members of the Field Club in the early 1880s, it is no surprise to find that William Waller was elected a member, probably in about 1890 and first contributed a paper to the proceedings of the Club in 1891. He was to continue his active involvement for over fifteen years. The membership soon rose to 400 and the Club established close links with the academic world and other institutions in this field.

Waller was an antiquarian and historian and although we know that he enjoyed his tours of the countryside, he was not qualified in any of the disciplines of natural history. His principal contributions to the Essex Field Club reflect the historic aspects of the land rather than the scientific aspects of its flora and fauna.

His first paper concerned the history of a fragment of Epping Forest: Monk Wood. In many ways this was one of his more important contributions, or at least Edward North Buxton thought so, as he added it as an appendix to the later editions of his guide to Epping Forest, first published in 1885 and which remains today one of the best of many guides to the Forest.

MONK WOOD IN LOUGHTON,
A FRAGMENT OF FOREST HISTORY

It needs to be remembered that Waller was writing this article one hundred years ago. Although pollarding the beeches, oaks and hornbeams, so well known in this area, had ceased at the time that the Corporation of London became Conservators, many of the trees had been pollarded in previous decades and still gave the appearance of stunted growth. Monk Wood today looks very different with one hundred years of growth, with nature having been left to its course and the great storms of the 1980s being responsible for most of the 'thinning'. It is only in very recent years that the Conservators have restarted pollarding on a small scale in a few selected areas none of which are at present in Monk Wood.

The history of Monk Wood goes back beyond the comparatively modern days of the parishioners of Loughton exercising their rights of lopping and the lord of the manor's right of fuel-assignments. At the beginning of the thirteenth century part of Loughton was called 'Luketon Snarringe', as being, or having been, the fee of Geoffrey Snarring. It appears that he had granted at any rate some portion of his estate to three owners, who held a certain wood in Luketon Snarringe in common, though their shares were not equal. The three owners were Geoffrey Renitot, Roger Fitz-Ailmar and Ralph de Assartis.

These three gentlemen decided to make a gift of the wood, fifty six and one half acres, to the Abbot and monks of the Abbey of Stratford Langthorne and to the Canons of the Holy Cross, Waltham Abbey. A further seventeen acres of wood and waste owned by Geoffrey Renitot and Roger Fitz-Ailmar were also given to the Canons of Waltham Abbey. The two Abbots, Henry of Waltham Abbey and Hugo of Stratford met to decide how the trees would be selected if either of them wished to fell any timber: the bailiff selecting four trees, with the Abbot of Stratford to have first choice of the first two and the Abbot of Waltham one of the remaining two, to reflect their respective shares in the wood.

The dissolution of the monasteries put an end to the Abbeys' ownership of the wood and we find that in 1582 Robert Wroth is owner and that in a report of a Committee appointed in that year to look into the felling of the wood, it is called 'Moncke Wood'. The article goes into some detail of the Committee's report. Waller uses as sources for his article Harleian MS 4809, the Duke of Lancaster's Surveys and Depositions, and a Forest Roll of Henry VII.

THE OLD TRACK FROM LONDON TO EPPING

The old main road from London to Epping ran through Chigwell, Abridge and Theydon Garnon. There was another route, Waller tells us, at any rate for travellers on horseback, as he learned from Pepys' Diary for 1659-60. Pepys was returning to London from Cambridge via Saffron Walden and spent a night at Epping. On the following morning he travelled through the Forest, east of Copped Hall Park and Woodridden, probably much in line with the existing road to the Wake Arms, at which point he bore off to the right to High Beach, near enough along the Wake Road or Verderers Ride of today. From there Pepys rode across Fairmead, past a house called 'Standing' and over Warren Hill to Buckhurst Hill. The remains of the house referred to as 'Standing' are believed to be embedded in the Warren House, now the residence of the Superintendent of Epping Forest.

Three hundred and fifty years later it is still possible to ride on horseback through the Forest from Epping (Bell Common) to Buckhurst Hill using Pepys' likely route and recounted by Waller almost one hundred and ten years ago.

SAKE'S (COMMONLY CALLED SNAKE'S) LANE, WOODFORD

One of Waller's shorter notes appeared in the transactions in 1892 and was followed up by a further note on the subject in 1893. He was often able to clarify points raised by other members on the vagaries of spelling and the corruption of place names. In this case he was able to prove that a man named Sake lived, and was once a landowner in Woodford. Waller found Sake's will proved in the Court of the Archdeacon of Essex on 2 October 1504. His supplementary note advises that he has now found an earlier mention of the Sake family in a Woodford Court Roll of Henry IV (1403-4). At that date the wives of John Sake senior and John Sake junior are described as being brewers. Waller found this Court Roll in the Public Record Office where he spent much of his time transcribing and translating MSS. However this piece of research was to little effect as the road is still today called Snake's Lane.

OLD LOUGHTON HALL

In a footnote the Editor of the transactions of the Field Club for 1893, says that:

'This paper almost purely historical and antiquarian, may be admitted into our pages, in as much as it relates to one of the most important of the Forest Manors. And further Mr Waller has collected so much original matter, not to be found in the county's histories, that we feel sure our readers will pardon this incursion into the preserves of our friends, the Essex Archaeological Society.'

The compliment to Waller was well justified. Several historians have written about Loughton Hall and the Wroth family but Waller must be credited with much of the detailed research. In this article he refers first to the period from Earl Harold, Godwin's son, down to the time of James I when the Manor of Loughton knew no resident lord. First the Canons of the Holy Cross at Waltham, and then, after the dissolution of the monasteries, the Kings and Queens of England, numbered it among their possessions. But it is probable that from very early times, the site of Loughton Hall was occupied by a manor house, which was inhabited by the lessees of the demesne.

It is not until 1602 that we come to any direct mention of Loughton Hall. The names of the Stonards and the Wroths now start to appear. A survey of the house in that year showed the house and other buildings in need of considerable repair. However, notwithstanding its condition, Sir Robert Wroth seems to have entertained his sovereign for two nights in July 1605. By 1612, when another survey was made, much of the house and buildings had been rebuilt. More than two centuries later an anonymous writer described the Hall as an Elizabethan pile of considerable beauty, the front and ceiling of the inner hall and a stone staircase being by Inigo Jones.

The manor remained in the possession of the Wroth family until 1738, when, on the death of Elizabeth, the childless widow of John Wroth, it passed to her great nephew, William Henry, fourth Earl of Rochford. It was sold by him in 1745 and henceforward passing by will, it became in 1825 the property of William Whitaker Maitland of Woodford Hall. Maitland carried out extensive alterations, both inside and out.

On Sunday, 11 December 1836 a fire broke out in the Library of the mansion. In a few seconds the whole of the west wing was one body of fire. The fire engine from Chigwell attended but the only supply of water was from a pond 360 yards away. The west wing was hopelessly burnt and the magnificent library of over 10,000 printed volumes and MSS was destroyed.

For many years the great iron gates, surmounted by the Wroth crest, kept guard over the foundations of the ancient house. In 1879, however, a new house designed by W Eden Nesfield, was built on the old site, by the Rev. John Whitaker Maitland. That house still stands but its future is currently under discussion by the local council who now own the building. Waller knew John Whitaker Maitland well and he was often able to provide historical documents and MSS to assist him in his researches.

TWO FOREST LODGES

Queen Elizabeth's Hunting Lodge remains one of the few buildings still existing in Epping Forest which is steeped in history, some true and some exaggerated. Waller was not the first to write about the building and several have followed him with equal distinction. In an article for the Field Club in 1893 Waller examines the report of the Special Commission appointed in 1589 to survey two houses in Waltham Forest. The members of the Commission were Robert Wroth, John Hill, Francis Stonerde, William Rowe, Francis Stacye and Edward Ellyot. One of houses was called Great Standinge, and is described as standing in or on Dannetts Hill, the other, called the Lodge is said to be situated in 'le Newe Lodge Walke' in the parish of Waltham Holy Cross.

The Commissioners' instructions were to inquire, in every way they were able, into the condition of the houses and the necessary costs of repairing them, and their report was to be delivered, written on parchment, and with as little delay as possible, to the Barons of the Exchequer at Westminster. Waller found the copy of the Commissioners' report in a somewhat decayed condition and with some gaps, but he felt that enough remained legible to make a transcript worth printing.

The Great Standinge is identified as Queen Elizabeth's Hunting Lodge and the report of the survey indicated the need for extensive repairs including:

> 'Walles and about the house to be plastered and mended'
> 'Mending the roof and kovering the same with tyle'
> 'A chimney of lome needs to be taken down because it annoyeth greatly and the building of a newe with repairing the Oven'
> 'Windows and flowers to be mended'
> 'Ffencing work'

The materials needed and quantities are shown.

A shorter list of repairs is shown for the other house or keeper's lodge situated in the New Lodge Walk. This is identified with the building known as Fairmead Lodge, which was in fact of much older origin than Queen Elizabeth's Lodge, having been built in the fourteenth century, although it no longer exists today. The article is

illustrated by two charming drawings of the buildings by
Henry Cole in 1893 when both buildings did exist.

In 1901 Waller received from a member of the Bath and
Cheltenham Archaeological Society a book written in the
fifteenth century which included a few references to
Essex. One of these is in the form of a Warrant from
Humphrey, Duke of Gloucester, who was Chief Warden of
the Forests South of the Trent, addressed to the Steward of
the Forest of Essex, instructing him to newly construct
without delay a lodge and a pimfold within the Forest for
the convenience of Ministers of my Lord the King. The
Warrant is dated 1444. Waller suggests that this might provide the initial instruction for the Great Standinge on
Dannetts Hill or possibly other lodges at Stratford or
Hainault. More recently, no less an authority than Sir
William Addison has dismissed this suggestion as far as the
Great Standinge is concerned, arguing that this building
was not completed until almost a hundred years later in
1543. However, the document is still an important one in
its own right.

Queen Elizabeth's Lodge, Chingford, looking south
(Drawn by H A Cole June 1893

DANNETTS HILL

In his article on Queen Elizabeth's Hunting Lodge, Waller referred to it being sited on Dannetts Hill and pondered the origin of the name Dannetts. He found reference in a Forest Roll of Henry VII's time to Danherst or Danhurst, being one of the woodwards of Chingford Walk. He suggests that Dannetts is merely a variant from the earlier Danhurst and was once the name of a part of the Forest between Chingford Walk (Hawk Wood) and Buckhurst Hill. However, in a note in the transactions in 1893, Waller has done some further research and come across a document of 1617 which refers to Dannymor Hill, alias Chingford waste. Half a century later Lady Elizabeth Botheby *(sic)* claimed to appoint a sworn woodward of all her woods, called Larks and Danhurst Hill.

THE EPPING HUNT

The story of the Epping Hunt has been told by both writers and poets over many years. Waller's interest is of a more legal nature as he was sent a manuscript of a 'Memorandum as to the right of the Citizens of London to hunt in its vicinity, including Epping Forest'.

The manuscript contains extracts from various ancient documents, with translations appended. The earliest is an undated letter in Saxon, addressed by Gostrigh, the Sheriff, to all citizens of London, telling them not to hunt unless by his command or order. This is followed by an extract from a Charter of Henry I, who in 1101 confirmed to the citizens of London their sporting rights, as enjoyed by their predecessors in Chiltern, Middlesex and Surrey.

The printed Hundred Rolls of 1275 are next cited and we find a jury of inquisition stating that citizens might run, with their dogs, at hares, foxes, rabbits and wild cats, as far as the bridge of Stanes, and the gate of the park of Enfield, and to Stratford-le-Bow and to Waltham Holy Cross. By 1598 we find the Lord Mayor and other members of the Corporation hunting at Havering and other places in the Forest of Waltham. However, a note is added that this only refers to a wood owned by the City and not over the Forest at large.

Fallow deer

In the time of Henry VIII the office of 'Common Hunt' (Huntsman) existed, whose responsibilities included keeping hounds. However, in the following two hundred years there appears to have been considerable criticism of the activities of 'Mr Common Hunt'. Finally in 1807 the Corporation passed a resolution abolishing the office of Common Hunt. Although the Huntsman ceased to exist, hunting continued until 1858 by which time such disorderly scenes occurred regularly that it was banned. In evidence to a Select Committee in 1863, George Palmer, a Verderer of Epping Forest, said that the Lord Mayor and Aldermen had, to his knowledge, exercised for fifty years the right of hunting and killing a stag once a year.

Waller concludes that the manuscript only confirms William Fisher's statement, in his book *The Forest of Essex,* that there is no legal documentary evidence to support the Corporation of London's right to hunt in the Forest as exercised on the occasion of the Epping Hunt or, as it was also known, the Easter Hunt.

THE BARCLAY-JOHNSTON MSS
AND PAPERS RELATING TO EPPING FOREST

In 1890 Waller read a short paper on the mass of pamphlets, papers and books, in manuscript and in print which the Field Club had received from the executors of Henry Ford Barclay, who had been one of the Commissioners appointed by the Epping Forest Act of 1871. One of the executors was Andrew Johnston who was a Verderer of Epping Forest. Waller was one of the two Honorary Librarians of the Field Club at this time, and he undertook to classify the documents and to archive the set in boxes and bound volumes. The article provides an invaluable list of what each box contained, and they were kept in the Club library which at that time was domiciled at Queen Elizabeth's Hunting Lodge.

SANDPIT PLAIN

Waller's knowledge of the Forest and its management are demonstrated in a short note in 1894 in which he comments on the state of the Clay Ride from Baldwins Hill across Sandpit Plain to the Epping New Road. The Clay Ride was constructed in an earlier part of the nineteenth century when the Lord of the Manor of Loughton enclosed a major part of the Forest and intended to build houses along the line of the Clay Ride. Fortunately the Epping Forest Act of 1878 and the subsequent Arbitration put an end to this and returned the enclosures to the Forest. However, the Clay Ride remained, as it does today.

William Cole, the Honorary Secretary of the Field Club, had commented in the minutes of a Forest ramble in April 1894 that:

'One improvement most heartily to be desired and strongly recommended to the Conservators would be the obliteration of this grievously ugly ride. It should be ploughed up and planted, so as to blot out for ever one of the most atrocious projects of vandalism ever conceived in detriment of a noble "open space", even in those dark ages of Epping Forest History, before the dawn of the Judgment of Sir George Jessel.'

Waller in a subsequent note agreed with Cole's comments and added some practical points in referring to the ride as a constant eyesore. Would it not be possible, he asks, to break up the ride's hideous rigidity and give it curves, with plantations of thorn, among which sapling oaks, beeches and hornbeams might be sprinkled? And would not it be possible to make the approach to the Forest from Baldwins Hill less formal and rectangular? Waller's own plan was to close the present entry from Baldwins Hill, 'which is utterly impassable in winter', and add a narrower fresh one, more or less diagonally, and on the curve through the grove of young growth which has sprung up. A hundred years since Waller made these comments and little if anything has changed. It is still not too late for the Conservators to follow up William Cole's and William Waller's ideas.

Waller's contribution to the Field Club was substantial. Apart from acting as one of its Honorary Librarians, he was also the Honorary Treasurer for six years from 1895 and was a member of the Committee for even longer. He contributed to the Club's transactions until 1904.

St Nicholas, Loughton, c 1790

FEBRUARY, 1891.

OUGHTON PARISH MAGAZINE.

S. John the Baptist.

Rev. J. WHITAKER MAITLAND, M.A., Rector.

Rev. C. A. WATSON, B.A., Curate.

Churchwardens.

Mr. PERCY LLOYD and Mr. T. J. CLEMENTS.

Sidesmen.

Mr. J. N. MARSHALL.	Mr. S. WILKS.
Mr. T. T. NUNN.	Mr. W. H. WRIGHT.

S. Mary the Virgin.

Rev. W. ALLEN, B.A., Vicar.

Churchwardens.

Mr. R. H. SHARP and Mr. ARTHUR MAYOR.

Sidesmen.

Mr. C. MORRIS.	Mr. J. KALE.
Mr. H. H. CLARKE.	Mr. E. A. MORRIS.
Mr. F. EDWARDS.	Mr. T. EDWARDS.

The Parish Magazine may be obtained from

Miss BARTON, Post Office.	Mr. LEECH, Golden Hill.
Miss BLOWS, High Road.	Miss GROUT, Baldwyn's Hill.

Annual Subscription, including postage, 2/6.

All communications to be addressed to THE EDITOR, S. Mary's Lodge.

ALFRED B. DAVIS, PRINTER, EPPING.

Loughton Parish Magazine, February 1891

6
THE ESSEX
ARCHAEOLOGICAL SOCIETY

Of all the societies in which William Waller took an active part, the Essex Archaeological Society was probably his greatest interest and took up most of his time.

An archaeological society had existed in Colchester since 1850 but within a couple of years it was clear that there was desire for a county society, and so it was that the Colchester Society merged with the newly formed Essex Society in 1852. Its first President was John Disney, a Fellow of the Royal Society and the founder of the Chair of Archaeology at Cambridge University. The Bishop of Colchester and the Lord Lieutenant of the County were proposed as the first Patrons of the Society. An early list of members includes many well known Essex family names from the Braybrookes, Buxtons and Gurneys to the Rounds, Courtaulds and Ruggles-Brises.

Waller was elected a member of the Essex Archaeological Society in 1891. He not only contributed many papers to the Society's proceedings but was active in recruiting new members to the Society. He became successively Honorary Receiver of Subscriptions, Auditor and Treasurer of the Society and was for many years a member of the Council. Some of the more important articles by Waller appearing in the Society's Transactions include:

SHIP-MONEY IN ESSEX 1634-1640

In 1900 Waller undertook some research into the form of taxation known as Ship-Money. Waller starts in 1634 with some notes by Secretary Coke who proposed a tax to build a fleet to guard the 'Narrows Seas', to be paid for by a tax on the port towns. The Attorney-General was prepared to go further and include the maritime counties as well as the towns in the tax but a Committee thought it safest to begin with the port towns.

For more than six years no Parliament had met and

the King had to decide how best to implement the tax. The King first issued a writ, dated 20 October 1634, to the bailiffs and other legal men of certain towns as well as to the Sheriffs of Suffolk and Essex, and called on them to provide a warship of seven hundred tons, two hundred and fifty men and other materials of war, by 1 March 1635, and to maintain the same for twenty-six weeks thereafter. The ship was to be at Portsmouth by the date named.

The writ gave the corporations power to levy and any persons proving rebellious could be sent to prison. By 28 March 1635, £2,446 had been received and by August £657 remained to be paid out of a total cost of £6,615. The levy was extended to the whole area of the county and under a writ issued on 14 August 1635 the contribution of Essex was fixed at £8,000. The Sheriff of Essex put in a declaration of the way in which the sum was to be paid by each corporate town and by each of the nineteen Hundreds. Inevitably there were some protests and a reluctance on the part of some inhabitants to pay. Theydon Garnon refused to pay on the ground that they owned no land, but were told that it was the King's pleasure that personal estate should contribute. By 1637 the whole county was assessed, excepting only two parishes.

Waller found a volume, containing more than a hundred and fifty pages, which gave full details of a levy in 1636 for another ship of eight hundred tons. The contributions of each town and Hundred are first summarised in the document and then the full list for each parish. Even in those days the arm of the Revenue was exceeding long! However, in 1641 the King abolished the tax.

SOME ACCOUNT OF THE CHURCH OF ST NICHOLAS AT LOUGHTON

Although there is no mention in Domesday Book of the existence of a church at Loughton, it is quite possible that there was one, even before the Conquest. If, however, that was not the case, there is no doubt that one was built and endowed within the century following it, for in the first charter of Henry II we find confirmed in 1177 to the canons regular of Waltham Abbey, 'Luketon with the church and shroudland, and their appurtenances'. A few years later the church at Loughton, with others, is said to be devoted to the use of the sacristy of the monastery.

Waller records a number of early benefactions to the church including those from Juliana Stokesby in 1383 and John Mablerthorpe, a former rector, in 1455. In 1532 we find the first of the Stonard/Wroth families making considerable bequests. The existence of a 'poore mens box' is revealed by a reference in 1568 when a testator bequeathed 12d to it. Little else is recorded until early in the eighteenth century.

In the year 1720, Holman, an Essex antiquary, paid a visit to St Nicholas and says that the church is small, the church and chancel being of one breadth with a north aisle belonging to both. Holman records the memorials enshrined in the church, with the conclusion that the Wroth family are buried in the vault in the north aisle, but with no memorials. We have the benefit of a watercolour drawing made in 1790 by David Thomas Powell who was born in 1771 of a well known Loughton family. Powell describes the church and refers to the chapel on the north side of the chancel including, against the walls, several hatchments of the Wroth family.

The next recorded visit to the church occurs in Ogborne's account of Loughton in the early nineteenth century, which records further memorial tablets. Writing in 1873, Mr J Perry gives an account of the church and says that at the end of the eighteenth century one bell was sold for repairing the church, the second bell bore the date 1621 and the founder's name, and the third bell bore the date 1655.

Waller regrets that the older records of the Loughton vestry are unfortunately extremely meagre, only one old volume (1720-1741) surviving. In 1739 we read that John Eyre was granted all right, title or interest in a pew in the church which his family had used for many years. This is the Eyre family which we have heard of already living at Slyders Gate on what is now the Uplands Estate, and after whom Waller named two semi-detached houses on Church Hill which he had built in 1904.

For some seven centuries the ancient church of St Nicholas stood on the site chosen by the earliest church builders in Loughton. But with the lapse of time, village life had moved to the fringes of the highway on what today is the road through Loughton from Buckhurst Hill to Epping. This change led to a wish for a more convenient site for the church and in 1846 the existing church of St John Baptist was consecrated and which stands close to the main road. Possibly due to an ill timed spirit of economy, the erection of the new church saw the demolition of the old one, with a resolution to transfer and remove all tombs, stones, monuments and monumental tablets to the new church. In fact only the brasses were removed from their slabs and transferred to the new church.

The chancel and part of the nave of the old church were left standing and new northern and western walls built up. However, in 1876 they were demolished and the existing Memorial Chapel was built by the mother of the then rector.

Waller reproduces a plan of the foundations of the old church showing the tombs and memorials which at the time he was writing (1916) could be identified in the existing churchyard but which now are mostly covered by grass and brambles, with the exception of the Purbeck Slab with three separate matrices which is the tomb of John Stonard and his two wives. Waller ends his article by saying that since the old church was demolished seventy years ago (now almost 160 years) it is still possible to experience a pang of regret at its uncalled for demolition. Current day historians will echo this view. Some of the stonework from the demolished church was used in the construction of the Church House at the new St John's.

Old Loughton Hall before the fire

A NOTE ON THE HUNDRED OF ONGAR

William Waller was not the first to give an account of the famous MS of the Ward-Staff Royal for the Hundred of Ongar. Philip Morant had over a century earlier given thanks for the author of this important sixteenth century document. Waller was able to look at the original MS which consisted of thirty-nine pages sewn together and somewhat damaged at the top but otherwise in good condition. The document starts with a copy of the Letters Patent, granting to one John Stoner, the bailiwick of Ongar and Harlow, with the office of ward-staff of the said Hundred.

The recital of the Letters Patent is followed by a list of the parishes and hamlets within the Hundred of Ongar, and a preamble stating that the book contains the names of the tenements and occupiers owing suit to the three weekly Hundred Court, the Sheriffs Tourn and the Leets and Law-days held of the same. Reference is next made to records made by Humfrey le Bohun, the Earl of Hertford and Essex and Constable of England, lord of the said liberties and Hundreths, added at Pleashy (Pleshey) in 1336.

Waller goes on to describe who attended each of the courts and for what purposes. For example, the tenants of Woolston Hall, in Chigwell, we are told, ought to repair a Trebechett (ducking stool), and also a bridge for carts called Hiends Bridge.

Waller finds it not quite easy to determine what precise object the compiler had before him in making the extracts from the Rolls. One's impression is, says Waller, that a new Steward finding himself without a Rental, set to work to compile one from the Rolls. Today's historians are grateful to him.

ESSEX FIELD NAMES

One task which took Waller much time to research was his compilation of Essex field names by Hundreds. Waller's objective was to collect and arrange systematically those which occur over the whole county. At first Waller thought that he would visit each parish and inspect the Tithe Commutation Award from which he would compile the list. However, he decided that this would be tedious and so he approached the Board of Agriculture, in whose custody the sealed copies of the various Awards were deposited. He managed to overcome some bureaucratic obstacles to this and was able to publish his first instalment covering field names in the Hundred of Ongar, and the Half Hundreds of Harlow and Waltham.

Further instalments appeared in the Society's Transactions over a number of months and on completion a bound volume was published.

A FOURTEENTH CENTURY PLURALIST:
RICHARD DE DRAX, RECTOR OF HARLOW

In September 1911 Waller read a paper, appropriately at a meeting at Harlow. Waller started his lecture by referring to two other Harlow clergy: Simon de Bruninton (rector 1234-35) and Adam Cacch (parson of Harlow in 1346), both of whom were not in Newcourt's *Repertorium* of 1710 and could now be added. The third name, found in the Calendars of Papal Registers, is Richard de Drax.

Waller, in his true Protestant fashion, prefaced his comments on Drax by finding it, 'well nigh incredible that the Popes should have arrogated to themselves, and practically secured, the right to appointment to benefices and church dignities of every kind in England' in the first half of the fourteenth century.

Drax was a Yorkshireman and a Doctor of Civil Law who had become an advocate in the Roman Court and then settled at Avignon. By 1353 he was Rector of Harlow, and probably before then in January 1352, a canon and prebend of Barneby in Howden (Yorks) although this was never confirmed. In September of the same year he obtained a provision of the canonry and prebend of Coleworth, Chichester, reserved to the Pope in the lifetime of Thomas de London.

In April 1354 Drax made application for the canonry and prebend of St Patrick's, Dublin and this request was granted. In October 1357 our rector prays for a canonry of York and prebend of Donington. The request was granted although the prebend appears to have been occupied by others. In December 1358 Drax applied with success for a canonry and prebend of Beverley (Yorks.)

Whether Drax intended to quit Avignon and return to England, there is no evidence to show. He was by now rector of Harlow, canon of Chichester, canon of Beverley, and an advocate in the Roman Court. However, in December 1359 he applied for and obtained the archdeaconry of Totnes. This last preferment rendered the new archdeacon somewhat uneasy as to his tenure of the rectory of Harlow and he persuaded the Archbishop of Auch to write a letter asking that he might be allowed to retain the rectory, which the Pope had willed him to resign. The request was granted but here matters became confused, as within a month in May 1360 the rectory was granted to two other persons!

Richard de Drax died sometime between August 1360 and April 1361 and by all accounts he retained the rectory at Harlow up until his death.

AN EXTINCT COUNTY FAMILY: WROTH OF LOUGHTON HALL

Elsewhere in this memoir I have commented on Waller's researches into old Loughton Hall and one of its occupants, Sir Robert Wroth. Waller was to investigate the history of the Wroth family in much detail and to publish his findings in three parts covering many pages of the Society's transactions. It would be invidious to try to summarise Waller's contribution to the history of this family and I can only refer any of today's historians who are interested in the subject to volumes VIII and IX of the *Transactions.* However the appended table shows the Pedigree of the Wroth family from the first half of the sixteenth century. This is the point at which Waller starts his discourse but other historians have carried the family history back to 1351 when Sir John Wroth was Sheriff of London and Mayor ten years afterwards.

FRIDAY HILL AND THE BOOTHBYS

The purpose of this short note, written in 1915, was to conjecture on the origin of the name of Friday Hill and to relate a little of the history of the Boothby family. Waller first dismisses any link between the name of the day of the week and Friday Hill. He comes to the conclusion that Friday was the surname of a man and cites a reference in 1589 to a messuage or tenement commonly called Fridayes Hill. The next mention of the place is found in the will of Thomas Botheby in 1625 with a reference to Fridaishill House, Chingford. Waller goes on to list the other details in the will of a family who continued to live in Chingford for several centuries.

Waller contributed many other articles, too long to list here, but mention should be made of some of them:

'Some additions to Newcourt's *Repertorium'*, based on notes prepared by J Challenor-Smith, which was an undoubted welcome addition to Essex parochial history.

'The Court Rolls of the Manors of Wethersfield and Wivenhoe', in the critical reign of Richard II, short but instructive studies.

'The transcription and editing of the Inventories of Church Goods in 1552 for the Hundreds of Uttlesford, Freshwell and Clavering.'

'Some Essex Manuscripts' belonging to Mr Chisenhale Marsh of Gaynes Park.

An extended series of articles on 'Old Chigwell Wills'.

A published volume on *The Feet of Fines for Essex.*

Following Waller's death in July 1917, a lengthy obituary by the President appeared in the Society's *Transactions.* He commented that from the day Waller was elected a member, he set himself to further its interests in every way and to increase its usefulness. He lived to see a remarkable development in its output of archaeological work, largely due to his own energy. He continued that Waller devoted himself more especially to the laborious transcription and careful editing of original records and MSS bearing on our local and family history, whether preserved at the Public Record Office, the British Museum, or Somerset House, or disinterred from the archives of Essex houses. Waller even wrote the Society's history for its Diamond Jubilee celebrations in 1912.

THE WROTH FAMILY PEDIGREE

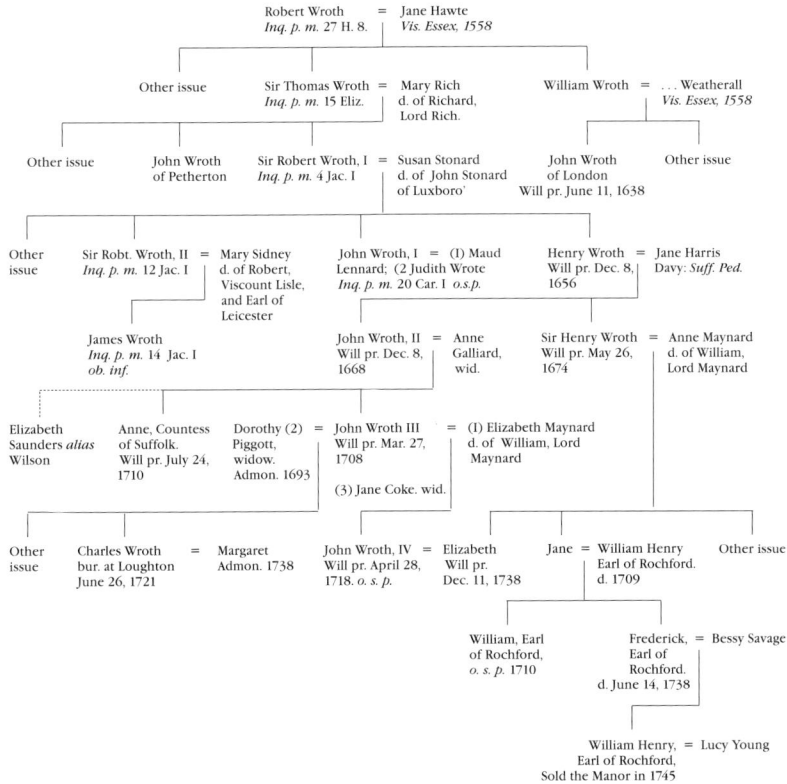

Robert Wroth = Jane Hawte
Inq. p. m. 27 H. 8. | *Vis. Essex, 1558*

Other issue

Sir Thomas Wroth = Mary Rich
Inq. p. m. 15 Eliz. | d. of Richard,
Lord Rich.

William Wroth = . . . Weatherall
| *Vis. Essex, 1558*

Other issue

John Wroth
of Petherton

Sir Robert Wroth, I = Susan Stonard
Inq. p. m. 4 Jac. I | d. of John Stonard
of Luxboro'

John Wroth
of London
Will pr. June 11, 1638

Other issue

Other
issue

Sir Robt. Wroth, II = Mary Sidney
Inq. p. m. 12 Jac. I | d. of Robert,
Viscount Lisle,
and Earl of
Leicester

John Wroth, I = (I) Maud
Lennard; (2 Judith Wrote
Inq. p. m. 20 Car. I *o.s.p.*

Henry Wroth = Jane Harris
Will pr. Dec. 8, | Davy: *Suff. Ped.*
1656

James Wroth
Inq. p. m. 14 Jac. I
ob. inf.

John Wroth, II = Anne
Will pr. Dec. 8, | Galliard,
1668   wid.

Sir Henry Wroth = Anne Maynard
Will pr. May 26, | d. of William,
1674   Lord Maynard

Elizabeth
Saunders *alias*
Wilson

Anne, Countess
of Suffolk.
Will pr. July 24,
1710

Dorothy (2) = John Wroth III
Piggott, | Will pr. Mar. 27,
widow.   1708
Admon. 1693

= (I) Elizabeth Maynard
d. of William, Lord
Maynard

(3) Jane Coke. wid.

Other
issue

Charles Wroth = Margaret
bur. at Loughton | Admon. 1738
June 26, 1721

John Wroth, IV = Elizabeth
Will pr. April 28, | Will pr.
1718. *o. s. p.*   Dec. 11, 1738

Jane = William Henry
Earl of Rochford.
d. 1709

Other issue

William, Earl
of Rochford,
o. s. p. 1710

Frederick, = Bessy Savage
Earl of
Rochford.
d. June 14, 1738

William Henry, = Lucy Young
Earl of Rochford,
Sold the Manor in 1745

Above: From Baldwins Hill, 26 September 1901
Below: The Forge Cottage, 1902

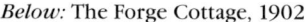

7
THE ESSEX REVIEW

The *Essex Review* was first published in January 1892 when it described itself as: 'an illustrated quarterly record of everything of permanent interest in the county'. In the first issue the Editor commented that Essex is peculiarly rich in local and personal associations, historical recollection and antiquities, social ties and history, though these may not have been so well elucidated, or the traditions so commonly observed and recorded, as in some other counties. Over the next century the *Essex Review* was to make a major contribution in rectifying this deficiency.

William Waller made his first contribution to the *Essex Review* in 1893 with a short note on the disastrous fire at old Loughton Hall, with particular reference to the practice of burning a beacon light at all seasons during the night, from a cupola at the top of the centre of the building. The light was visible for miles in all directions, and the practice probably had its origin in a hospitable desire to direct night-overtaken travellers to a place of safety and rest.

Longer articles soon followed together with further short notes, including those on 'An Essex Alchemist' (Sir Thomas Elys), 'The Abbots of Waltham in the Papal Registers' (researched from eight volumes of *Calendars of Papal Registers* in the fourteenth century), and a 'Historical Note on Monkhams'.

The following articles give further examples of Waller's interests in local history and his painstaking research:

THE FORESTERS' WALKS IN WALTHAM FOREST

With views from his house over Epping Forest and as a keen walker and bicyclist throughout the forest, Waller found much to interest him in its history. 'The Forester, or keeper of the King's wild beasts, was sworn to execute his office in his Walk of the forest, to be of good behaviour himself to the King's wild beasts and the vert of the forests, and not to conceal the offence of any other person, either in vert or venison, done within his charge.' Here Waller is quoting from William Fisher's authoritative work on the history of the laws and administration of the Forest of Essex, published in 1887 and still the definitive work on the subject. Both Fisher and Waller were barristers and they may possibly have met, having such common interests, although Fisher lived at Guildford in Surrey.

By the middle of the seventeenth century there were nine Walks in Waltham Forest: Loughton, Woodford, Epping, New Lodge, Chingford, Chappel Hainault, Leyton, West Hainault and Walthamstow. A map drawn in about 1641 accompanies the article showing the extent of each Walk. A tenth Walk, that of Lambourne and Chigwell was added sixty years later by dividing Loughton Walk.

Waller goes on to describe in more detail the limits of each Walk. Of New Lodge Walk he adds that it has been so named perhaps since the days of Richard II in the first year of whose reign Alan de Buxhull had a grant, during pleasure, of the custody of the King's new lodge, without rendering anything therefore, but he is to keep in repair the houses of the said lodge. The lodge was finally demolished by the Conservators in 1898, by which time little if any of the original lodge remained and the buildings were in a very dilapidated condition, having been used during the second half of the nineteenth century as a Retreat – a place for refreshments.

It was, however, still to be regretted that the Corporation of London decided on this rare occasion that history was not worth preserving. The site of New Lodge was immediately next to the old Fairmead Oak, now also no more, on Fairmead Plain. Fortunately many photographs and drawings of the Lodge still exist.

The remaining part of Waller's article is taken up with a set of returns made by the under-keepers in the years 1663-1670 in which they report on the number of deer in each Walk, those killed by 'His Majesty's Hounds' during the Hunt, and other deer caught as fee (gifts) deer for various Government officials and forest officers, including the Verderers, although they no longer have that privilege today.

LUXBOROUGH IN CHIGWELL

The manor, or farm, of Luxborough has a long history. Waller is in his element here, tracing in detail the ownership from the fourteenth century when William de Longtheburg gave 100 marks in silver to Henry de Doule and Eve, his wife, for a messuage, 122 acres of arable land, 6 acres of meadow, 4 acres of woodland and rents amounting to 6s 4d in the parish of Chigwell. In 1558 John Stonard, grandson of that well known Loughton farmer bought Luxborough. By this time the extent of the land had changed somewhat, being described as including 20 acres of arable, 100 acres of meadow, 100 acres of pasture and an acre of woodland. Norden, writing in 1594 classifies as 'fayre' the house which he says was built by 'J Stonerde'. In 1580 Stonard had died and left the house first to his wife and then on her decease to his son-in-law and daughter Robert and Susan Wroth.

At the beginning of the eighteenth century we find that Robert Knight, cashier of the South Sea Company, is the new owner and has built a fine new house which was afterwards seized and sold by the Company, Sir Joseph Eyles being the purchaser. On Sir Joseph's death in 1740, Mr Knight repurchased it and dying four years later was succeeded by his son who was later to become Lord Luxborough. The latter half of the eighteenth century saw the house change ownership more than once with James Crockatt, Sir Edward Walpole, Mr Samuel Peach and Admiral Sir Edward Hughes in occupation. At sometime before 1819 the estate had been acquired by James Hatch of Claybury who pulled down the house and annexed the land to his own demesnes.

A drawing of the east front of the house, at the time of Sir Edward Hughes' occupation in 1796, is included in the article and shows a very grand Corinthian style mansion. Writers more recent than Waller have further researched the mansion and other records have come to light. The history of the house is more fully documented in the *Victoria History of the County of Essex*.

THE DEER IN WALTHAM FOREST 1588-1591

The main sources of Waller's article are the returns of the Court of Attachments, otherwise known as the Court of the Verderers, which met once in forty days and at which certain minor trespasses were dealt with summarily. For the most part, however, the presentments of attachments made by the Foresters were merely enrolled and returned to the Swainmote, which was held three times a year. This higher Court, to which jurors were summoned, certified as to facts and fixed the appropriate fines, but it was left to a yet higher, the Court of Justice Seat, presided over by the Chief Justice of the Forests, to decide as to whether an offence had been committed, and if so, what should be the punishment of the offender.

During the period December 1588 and June 1591 four hundred and thirty eight head of deer are accounted for in three Walks: Hainault, Chapple Hainault and Leyton. Of these many were killed and given away, but the casualties among the herds, especially among the fallow deer, and during the earlier months of the year, were heavy. The number of fee deer was high: even the French Ambassador received a fat buck! It was clear that the herds would soon be reduced to zero if the number of deer killed and given away continued at the rate of 1588. The returns to the Court of Attachments quoted by Waller show a continuation of the high losses of deer in the following years.

In a supplementary note in a later Quarterly Review Waller quotes some even earlier returns which he found in the British Museum. These include those for the years 1237-38. The returns are in Latin but this presented no problem to Waller, who was used to translating such manuscripts.

SOME ANCIENT CHARITIES

This is a short note by Waller of some benefactions in Essex which struck him as quaint and characteristic and which he obtained from the report of the Charity Commissioners for 1818-1837. Included in the list are:

A charity established at Clavering in 1537 was still distributed in 1836 in the form established by the donor, who had charged a house and lands called Valence, with the provision of a barrel of white and a cade of red herrings, yearly. The two barrels of herrings were sent to the house of the parish clerk in Lent, and distributed in the church by him and the sexton, four fish being given to each married couple, two to each widow or widower, and one to each child.

At Colne Engaine there is an acre always held by the sexton and is called Sexton's Orchard.

At Saffron Walden the rules of the almshouses called by the name of King Edward VI are somewhat severe, and are vigorously expressed. Any inmate offending against them is ' to be expelled and put out for the first fault, as a caterpillar or destroyer of the commonwealth of the said house'.

MORE ESSEX PLACE NAMES

In an article in October 1911 Waller cited three examples of the corruption of original names. In the parish of Theydon Bois there is a wood shown on the map as Red Oaks Wood. When the Epping Forest Commission was sitting (1871-1876) and some learned lawyer enquired of the oldest inhabitant whether he knew the existence of such a place, the reply received was in the negative. Try him with 'Ruddocks' said the steward of the manor, who was sitting hard by. To the question as amended the answer came pat, 'yes I know Ruddocks'. Red Oaks is merely a modern etymologised version of the name of one the tenants of the Manor in 1323, a Thomas Ruddock, to whom the wood may have belonged, or against whose holding it lay.

Again in Theydon Bois we find Thrift Hall, the genesis of which is curious. Many long years ago a wood, known as Theydon Frith, extended from the village green possibly to the marshlands by the Roding. In the course of time the wood was stubbed and converted into arable use; the name *frith* still clung to the land, but the wood had passed out of use and conveyed no meaning. Thrift, on the other hand, was a known word, with a meaning, and, so it took the place of frith. A little later and a 's' was added; 14 acre Thrifts and Boggy Thrifts marked two fields; while Thrift Wood stood to remind men of the ancient *frith*. Then some one came along, built a house, and, regarding Thrifts as the possessive form of a surname, called his house Thrifts Hall. Frith Hall or Wood Hall, would have been more apposite.

The third example refers to a wood in the parish of Stondon Massey called Mellow Purgess. In seeking the origin of the name, Waller looked at the Tithe Map which gave Mal y perdu, which tradition rendered *mal eau perdu,* accounting for it by some tale of a Norman knight who came to grief at the spot. Waller then found some sixteenth century documents which made mention of a grove called Malepardus. Here he finds a possible literary connection with Maleperdays, the stronghold of Master Reynard, the hero of the popular Beast epic of the Middle Ages. (Waller went into more detail in an article in the transactions of the Essex Archaeological Society in 1905).

HOPPIT

In one of his earlier notes (October 1894) Waller entered into a discussion on the derivation of Hoppit. (Little was he to know that a hundred years later the small housing development at the southern boundary of Ash Green was to be called Waller's Hoppet.) Waller first points out that the word may be spelled 'hoppit' or 'hoppet', and that he always regarded it as a diminutive of the Anglo-Saxon 'hope', a meadow. He found one or two examples of the latter locally, such as Bushy Hope in Chingford, Arsward Hope in Chigwell and Swans Hope in Loughton.

However, in his review of all the Tithe Commutation awards for Essex he found that references to 'hoppets' in all cases are legion, being prefixed with a personal, and sometimes a local name, eg Garden hoppet, Hither hoppet, Carter's hoppet. Another correspondent ventured that 'hoppet' was the name given to a small square grass enclosure, consisting of a couple of roods. Further north in the Eastern Counties the alternative term 'pightle' is used more often.

BARNABY RUDGE AND CHIGWELL

The link between Chigwell and the inn described as the Maypole in Dickens' *Barnaby Rudge* had been debated in previous issues of the *Essex Review*. William Waller added a further note in April 1912, following the publication of the neat little King's Head Handbook, prepared in the main, Waller believed, for American visitors. The booklet included a paragraph about the fire described in *Barnaby Rudge:*

'It was four years earlier, in December 1836, that Loughton Hall perished in flames, and the sad tale of its destruction probably impressed itself on the imagination of Charles Dickens on the occasion of his previous visits to Chigwell, when the story of "the bright and vivid glare which illuminated all the country" could hardly fail to be often on the lips of those who had seen it. And there is no doubt that when Dickens speaks of the Warren he had Loughton Hall in mind; and, as no other building meets the requirements of the situation, we may confidently say, with Joe Willett, that "he means the great house naturally and of course. The old red-brick house, sir, that stands in its own grounds" – on the other side of the valley, he might have added.'

Following Waller's death the Review commented that he was: ' a scholar to whom the *Essex Review* owed much, few of our volumes are without short notes and short papers by him on the local and family history of his neighbourhood. All these were the results of original research pursued at the Record Office or among privately owned documents.'

The Essex Review (courtesy of *Essex Journal*)

8
THE HUGUENOT SOCIETY
OF LONDON

In 1889 Waller was elected a Fellow of the Huguenot Society of London, which had been formed in 1885. His interest in the Huguenots probably arose from his close friendship with William Minet, who was an old college friend. Minet's ancestors had escaped from France at the time of the revocation of the Edict of Nantes and had fled to England. William Minet published in 1892 the history of his family and in the preface to that book he mentions Waller: 'whose assistance has been constant and varied'. Waller and Minet were to work together and individually on many papers and books for the Huguenot Society over the next thirty years.

If Minet was the catalyst in interesting Waller in the Huguenot Society, Waller needed no introduction to Protestantism. He was, as we shall see later, an active member of St John's Church in Loughton and was strongly against the introduction of any High Church or 'Roman practices' in the services at St John's.

In introducing the transcripts of the Registers of one of the French Churches in London, it may only be coincidence that Waller quotes that other well known Essex ecclesiastical historian, John Strype. Strype (1643-1737) was appointed in 1669 to the perpetual curacy of Theydon Bois, which adjoins Loughton, before he moved to Leyton where he was to spend the next sixty-eight years. Strype was to end his days living in Hackney where of course Waller had been born. Strype was the son of a Brabantine refugee who set up business as a silk merchant in Houndsditch. In 1720 Strype summarised succinctly the legacy of the Huguenot refugees in London:

'The North West Parts of this Parish (Spittle Fields and Parts adjacent) of later times became a great harbour for poor Protestant Strangers, Walloons and French: Who as in former days, so of late, have been forced to become Exiles from their own Country for their Religion, and for the avoiding cruel Persecution. Here they have found Quiet and

Security, and settled themselves in their several Trades and Occupations, Weavers especially. Whereby God's Blessing surely is not only brought upon the Parish *(Come ye Blessed of my Father, &c. For I was a Stranger and ye took me in)* but also a great Advantage had accrued to the whole Nation, by the rich manufactures of weaving of Silks and Stuffs and Camlets: Which art they brought along with them. And this benefit also to the Neighbourhood, that these Strangers may serve for patterns of Thrift, Honesty, Industry and Sobriety, as well.'

EARLY HUGUENOT FRIENDLY SOCIETIES

In 1900 Waller read a paper at one of the Society's ordinary meetings on 'Early Huguenot Friendly Societies'. This was subsequently published in the Huguenot Society's *Proceedings* (vol VI) and remains one of the more important papers on the subject. Waller looked into the records of five friendly benefit societies of Huguenot origin in the East End of London. Waller argued that Friendly Societies owed their origin to the 'burial club' – the funeral was ever the occasion for a feast, but that care for the living as well as the dead was an obligation of the Guilds. As aliens the Huguenot refugees had no claim on the poor rate. The Huguenot Friendly Societies were mainly formed in the early part of the eighteenth century and were recognised formally by Act of Parliament in 1793.

Membership of the Society of Parisians, which was formed in 1687, was open to Protestants from the Paris region, aged between 18 and 41 years, and who lived within three miles of Christ Church, Spitalfields. An entrance fee of 2s 6d was payable with contributions of 1s per month. Benefits of 8s per week were payable during sickness, but limited to 52 weeks after which 4s was paid. £5 was paid for funeral expenses. Contributions and benefits changed over the years.

The Norman Society was formed in 1703 with an entrance fee of £2 but with weekly contributions of 1d. Benefits of 7s per week were payable but the Secretary and Treasurer had to visit the sick each week. Pensioners were paid 5s per week. The Society held its meetings (in1800) at the Weavers Arms in Brown Lane, Spitalfields. A case was reported in 1795 when a member had contributed £24 5s and had received £290 9s by the time of his death in La Providence Hospital. A few more similar cases and the Society would have ceased to exist. For this reason, most Societies related the amount of benefit to their capital from time to time.

The Society of Lintot was formed in 1708 at Phoenix Street, corner of Farthing Street at the sign of the Magpie. In 1824 membership was extended to the descendants from the whole province of Normandy, although preference was given to those from the Lintot district. Numbers were limited to 60.

Similar arrangements applied to the Society for High and Low Normandy, formed in 1764 and the Friendly Society, formed in 1720. All the Societies met at inns and in the second half of the nineteenth century, four out of five of the above Societies met at the Norfolk Arms in Ivimey Street.

Waller concluded by saying that these small Huguenot Societies have profited by their experience (of Societies that had gone bankrupt) and had modified themselves from time to time, gradually accumulating capital, and had formed the model on which the large Friendly Societies of today (1900), with their invested millions have been built up.

In 1907 Waller produced a supplement to his paper giving details of a Friendly Society formed in Dublin in 1719. However, this appears more in the nature of a Charitable than a Friendly Society. Nearer to his home Waller was involved with the Loughton Mutual Labor-Aid Society between 1891-1899.

REGISTERS OF THE FRENCH CHURCHES

The Huguenot Society since its inauguration in 1885 published a series of volumes of transcriptions of the Registers of French Churches, principally those in England. Waller and William Minet made major contributions to this series. (Minet has been followed by his daughter Susan in this research.)

THE PROTESTANT CHURCH AT GUISNES

The first volume in this series, with which Waller became involved, jointly in this case with Minet, was the transcription in 1891 of the Registers of the Protestant Church at Guisnes in France from 1668-1685. The reason why they chose a Protestant church in France, whereas their other work related to French churches in England, probably lies in the fact that Minet's ancestors, going back for two hundred years or longer, had lived in the Calais region near Guisnes and thus there was a family connection. Guisnes, familiar to some Englishmen as the scene of the historic splendour of the Field of the Cloth of Gold, was at the time of the Revocation of the Edict of Nantes, the religious centre of Protestantism in the north east of France.

At Guisnes the adherents of the 'Religion Pretendue Reformee' were permitted the free exercise of their form of worship. They had their own church and came from the villages round about and sometimes from towns not so near, to be married, to be baptised and to bury their dead. It is believed that the Church at Guisnes was built between 1598-1602 and it is probable that its erection followed on the promulgation of the Edict of Nantes in 1598. However, this building could only have been of a temporary character, and was succeeded by a much larger one, built about 1625. The importance of Guisnes as the centre of Protestantism in the district must have increased immensely after the destruction of a sister church at Marck in 1641.

Adjoining the Church was the Consistory which perhaps also served as the residence for the Minister. The Church existed until 1685, when by virtue of a decree, which preceded the actual revocation of the Edict, it was closed. The last entry in the Register of any ceremony at Guisnes is dated 26 June 1685. In October 1685 came the Revocation and shortly afterwards the Church was pulled down. It was alleged that in 1685 at a celebration of Communion, 10,000 persons had been present. However, Waller finds it difficult to accept these figures as entirely without exaggeration based on the number of entries in the Church Register.

Waller's own copy of the transcription of the Register still exists and contains some manuscript additions and amendments to place names in an appendix.

THE FRENCH CHURCH KNOWN AS
LA PATENTE IN SPITTLEFIELDS

In 1898 Waller again collaborated with Minet in editing the Registers of the Church known as La Patente in Spittlefields from 1689-1785. The French Church in the east of London was, like another in west London, familiarly known as La Patente. The origin of the name lies in the Letters Patent of 1688 under authority of which both churches were founded. The enrolment of the Letters Patent shows that they were not issued for the special case of the church in Spittlefields, but gave a several licence to an incorporated body of French ministers, with perpetual succession, to hire rooms, acquire land, build churches, and exercise their peculiar form of ecclesiastical discipline within the City of London and the suburbs. The congregation met first in Glovers Hall and two entries among the marriages in the Register (25 August and 13 October 1689) bear out this statement. This Hall, in which some of the synods of the French Churches are said to have been held, stood in Glovers Hall Court, on the south side of Beech Lane in Cripplegate Ward Without. Beech Lane still exists, connecting White and Red Cross Streets.

The heading of the third volume of the Registers, which opens on 21 August 1707, states that the congregation then met in Paternoster Row. Paternoster Row lay immediately south of Spitalfields market. In 1716 a lease of a chapel in Crispin Street was taken for thirty two years. Crispin Street still exists and runs north and south, on the west side of Spitalfields market. On expiry of this lease a chapel in Brown's Lane was purchased, and the first baptism is noted as having taken place in this building on 13 April 1740. In 1786 the congregation, together with an adjoining one known as Artillery, was finally merged in the London Walloon Church.

Waller and Minet note in the introduction to their transcription the difficulties caused by vagaries in the spelling of proper names. However, they provide a useful table of French place names for the origin of members of the congregation with a summary which shows that well over three-quarters of entries in the Registers relate to refugees and their descendants from the Poitou and Normandie districts. There is a similar table identifying all the streets in the City of London and East End in which the congregation lived. A further table shows an analysis of the trades of the persons in the Registers with not surprisingly weavers predominating.

THE FRENCH CHURCH AT THORPE-LE-SOKEN

The village of Thorpe-le-Soken lies about twelve miles east of Colchester in Essex. In 1912 the Huguenot Society of London published Waller's transcription of the Register of the French church there from 1684-1726. Waller also published separately a short history of the church but much of this is also contained in his introduction to the Registers.

In June 1683 the Bishop of London, who was very friendly to the refugees, gave to Jean Severin, a pastor, a commission to go to Beaumont, a village also near Colchester, and preach in the Anglican church there to the French Protestants, whom the persecution in France had caused to gather in the district. On the afternoon of 1 July he preached in the church, but the parishioners objected, on the grounds that they were thereby hindered from having the two services to which they were accustomed on Sunday. The French on their side, thought that it would be much more convenient to meet at Thorpe and made a petition to that effect to the Bishop. The Bishop gave his approval and also encouraged the local clergy not to make any difficulties in the matter.

Pastor Severin preached in the church at Thorpe on 29 July 1683 and undertook to fulfil the duties of the evangelical ministry in accordance with the canons and constitutions of the Anglican church. The congregation increased but it was two years later before it was decided to endeavour to obtain the Bishop's permission to build a chapel for the French refugee congregation. The Bishop approved the project, advised that the lord of the manor should be asked to give a site, and promised a licence. After a number of difficulties had been overcome a site was purchased in 1685 but it was not until 4 March 1688 that the first service was held in the new building. It appears that by 1726 most of the French congregation spoke English sufficiently to attend the (Anglican) Parish church, and in 1730 it was decided that there was no further use for the chapel. There was a subsequent proposal that it should be used as a schoolroom but this was never implemented and, by 1755, the chapel was demolished.

Waller tried to identify some of the descendants of the families in the original Registers but found very few. He also completed editing the Registers of the Dutch church at Colchester which had been started by Mr Moens.

EXTRACTS FROM THE COURT BOOKS OF THE WEAVERS' COMPANY

In 1914 Waller undertook some research into extracts from the Court Books of the Weavers' Company 1610-1730. He records in the introduction to this volume that:

'The records of the Weavers' Company of London, so many of them as have escaped the ravages and vicissitudes of times, have for some thirty years found a haven of rest and security in a strong room built for them in the Company's Almshouses at Wanstead in Essex. Leave having been granted to our Council to examine these records, and Wanstead being within convenient reach of my home, I offered to make the examination and record the results.' [The Almshouses still exist.]

Although Waller completed his researches, the volume was not published by the Huguenot Society until 1931 and then under the editorship of William Minet.

In an obituary in the proceedings of the Huguenot Society for 1917, Waller's death is recorded for special mention: 'by reason of the many and valuable services he had rendered to the Society during the twenty eight years that he had been a Fellow of it.' Waller had been a Vice-President of the Society and had served several terms as a member of the Council, a position which he held at the time of his death.

Committee and Judges at Loughton Horticultural Show in 1906

9
SOCIETY OF ANTIQUARIES
IN LONDON

In March 1892 Waller was elected a Fellow of the Society of Antiquaries. A search of the proceedings of the Society does not show that he contributed any papers specifically for the Society, although their library at Burlington House contains copies of several of Waller's papers written for other Societies and, of course the Society was the recipient of copy No 11 of *Loughton in Essex.*

It is most probable that Waller regularly attended meetings of the Society in London. His friend William Minet was also a member and was its Treasurer for many years. The only record of Waller participating in the Society's proceedings is as a scrutineer at the annual ballot for the election of officers in 1915-1917.

Waller must, however, have been highly regarded within the Society as, following his death in July 1917, an obituary appeared in the following year's proceedings which spoke of:

'Another serious loss was the death on 28 July 1917 of Mr W C Waller, who was elected a Fellow of our Society in 1892. He was for long engaged on two laborious undertakings relating to Essex antiquities. One of these was a systematic collection under Hundreds of Essex Field-names, transcribed from the Tithe Commutation Awards. The other entitled 'some additions to Newcourt's Repertorium', was an important contribution to the parochial history of the county. Many papers of his on local history are included in the Transactions of the Essex Archaeological Society, including one on the extinct Wroth family of Loughton Hall. He devoted himself with great industry to the transcription and careful editing of original records bearing on local matters and the volume on Essex Fines was due to his initiative and superintendence. In 1891, in collaboration with our Treasurer, Mr W Minet, he transcribed and edited the Registers of the Protestant church at Guisnes, and in 1898 the Register of the church known as La Patente in Spitalfields.'

St John's Church, Loughton, in c 1896

10
ST JOHN'S CHURCH LOUGHTON

The local churches in England have always provided a rich source of information for the history of a local area and its inhabitants. William Waller was able to benefit from this in writing his history of Loughton and the other articles that he contributed to the Essex Field Club, the Essex Archaeological Society and the *Essex Review.* His note on the history of the first church in Loughton, St Nicholas, and his summary of many of the wills of prominent residents were both assisted by researches into church records.

With Waller we have the additional benefit that he was during his time in Loughton a very active member of the church. Apart from the religious aspects of the church, the church Vestry, until late in Victorian times, also carried out many of the duties of the modern District Council including appointing Overseers for the Poor, Highway Surveyors and Reeves. This was all faithfully recorded in the Vestry Minute Book and the original minute book covering the period 1869 to 1908 for the Loughton Vestry now resides in the Waller archive at the Essex Record Office.

THE LOUGHTON VESTRY

Waller regularly attended the meetings of the Vestry and it is noted in the minutes that for a number of years he audited the accounts of the Parochial charities. In 1870 the Vestry agreed to propose that a new church should be built at the southern end of the parish and thus St Mary's came to be built. Much of the cost of the new church was raised by donations from the parishioners of St John's but interestingly both William Waller and his aunt Jane made gifts including a marble credence table and the lectern instead of money.

A sample agenda from the Vestry meeting of 4 April 1892 shows the following items:

> Nomination of Churchwardens
> Accounts for Allotment Grounds
> Overseers' nominations

Assessor's appointment
Road Surveyor's Report
Sanitary Committee
Burial Board
Appointment of Reeve

In connection with the Surveyor's Report to the meeting, Waller asked about two obstructions on York Hill, namely a fence which projected and also a wall. It was decided that the fence should be removed but the wall had to stay.

RECTORS OF LOUGHTON

At the time Jane Miller Waller and William Waller moved to Loughton in the early 1870s, John Whitaker Maitland had already been Rector for almost twenty years and was to remain Rector until 1910. They were to become close friends and we find notes in diaries and see from letters between them that Maitland would often call on the Wallers at Ash Green. Maitland was also very helpful to Waller in providing information for him on his historical researches.

Maitland was also Lord of the Manor of Loughton with as such the right to appoint his successor as Rector. Shortly before he died in 1910, Maitland offered the living to the Revd Arthur Montford, who introduced a more catholic pattern of worship.

CONSISTORY COURTS

The changes introduced by the new Rector did not please all the congregation and a number of influential people, led by William Waller, protested against the practices. Waller was subsequently to prepare some extended notes on the events that took place between 1910 and 1914, putting his side of the argument, and we also have the benefit of some notes believed to have been written by Montford with his case.

Waller's notes start with a useful summary of events:

'The Revd John Arthur Montford was instituted at St John's on 7 April 1910. He made some alterations and at evensong the candlesticks were lighted and extinguished before the sermon. On 20 May 1910 the brass cross was replaced by a marble crucifix, with on 25 December two Flemish candlesticks. On 12 February 1911 a small brass crucifix was permanently set up.

On Saturday 30 March 1912 the Bishop of Colchester dedicated the completed reredos, and on Sunday we found six great Flemish candlesticks on the retable, four having been added. Vestments (coloured) were introduced some time before. In February 1913 the times of the services had been altered and a formal remonstrance was signed by eighty people.

I had withdrawn to St Mary's when the four additional candlesticks were set up, this being the last straw.'

In March or April 1912 Waller wrote to the Registrar of the Diocese asking whether he was in order to apply for a Faculty for the removal of the four additional candlesticks on the retable. Waller gave four reasons for their removal. The Registrar responded that it was open to Waller to apply for a Faculty. However, several members of the congregation had withdrawn to St Mary's and those who remained seemed contented, so Waller decided to discontinue his proceedings.

Early in 1913 it appears that as a result of the changes to the times of services, eighty parishioners, headed by the Churchwardens, made an unsuccessful protest to the Rector against the innovations that he had introduced. Waller decided to take up again the issue of the candlesticks and crucifix, and submitted a petition to the Chancellor of the Diocese. The Rector, this time with the support of the Churchwardens, submitted his case justifying the changes, to which Waller responded at length.

A Consistory Court was held by the Chancellor of the Diocese of St Albans (Loughton was in the Diocese of St Albans for a short time before the see of Chelmsford was established) on 28 November 1913 to hear the arguments. The Chancellor decided that the figure on the cross had to be removed and the number of candlesticks must be reduced to the original two. (Montford commented in his notes that the case took four hours to hear and they missed lunch!) A Faculty ordering the removal was issued, dated 6 January 1914.

It should be said that the basis of the Chancellor's judgment was that the Rector had failed to follow church procedure and to obtain the Vestry's approval and a Faculty to his proposed changes prior to carrying them out, rather than on the merits of the changes. Thus on a legal point he had to agree with the complainants.

The Rector's case was also weakened as he had applied for and obtained a Faculty in March 1912 when he removed the existing Communion table and replaced it with a table of cedar and oak, with panels of alabaster and mosaic inlays at the front and side.

Waller's case and Montford's reply both relied to some extent on ecclesiastical law as they each interpreted it. Montford in his notes on events adds that at a meeting of the Vestry in April 1912, a vote of thanks was carried unanimously congratulating the Rector on the additions to the East End of the church, and that Waller had been present and had said nothing. Waller had audited the accounts for the cost of the alterations and additions and had said nothing when discussing them with Montford. The Archdeacon and Rural Dean had visited the church and expressed themselves pleased with what had been done.

The Consistory Court case of 1913 was widely discussed in both local and national newspapers and in the Church press. Within little more than a year Montford announced that he was moving to a larger parish in North London and he left Loughton in 1915.

THE PARISH MAGAZINE

Waller's principal contribution to the Parish Magazine was of course the instalments of his history of Loughton which were to become his book *Loughton in Essex.* However, one other notable contribution in 1900 was the marriage records for Loughton from 1675 to 1812. Waller had transcribed the baptisms, marriages and burials for the parish of Loughton from the registers held at the British Museum. These registers included some additional information about the parish church and Waller notes an inventory of articles belonging to the church and submitted for the inspection of J Hugh Chambers Jones, Archdeacon of Essex, at the visitation on 18 June 1832.

Waller decided to print those related to marriages solemnised at Loughton, Essex. The list provides a useful record of many of those names which have been referred to by Waller in his perambulations of Loughton, including Thomas Wignall who married Sarah Brewer in May 1681, William Clay and Sarah Wheeler in December 1700, John Wroth and Mrs Jane Coke in November 1706, and William Tunnridge and Anne Bridge in May 1716.

In 1895 Waller wrote an account of St John's Church at the time of its Golden Jubilee. The account relates mainly to the decision to erect a new church, the various sites considered, the cost and funding of the church and the award of the building contract.

A list of benefactions to the parish of Loughton had first been published in the Parish Magazine in 1893. This summarised the various charities, some of which had originated in the sixteenth century and possibly earlier, and included the Whitaker charities. The list had been updated in 1898 and Waller was to further update it in 1915.

WALLER MEMORIALS

Mention has already been made of the brass memorial in St John's to Waller's son Geoffrey and to the Lych Gate as a memorial to his daughter Vera. Following his death in 1917 a brass memorial to William Chapman Waller was placed in the north apse under the window dedicated to St Nicholas and below that for his son. William Waller, his wife, his aunt and the four children are all buried in the family tomb in the churchyard.

The Church of St. John the Baptist, Loughton.
No. 1084.

Altar of St John's Church, Loughton, 1905

11
OTHER LOCAL INTERESTS

The amount of time and enthusiasm which Waller expended on his historical researches for the Essex Field Club, the Essex Archaeological Society and the Huguenot Society would leave little time for most people to pursue other interests. Waller, however, found time to become involved locally in two or three organisations apart of course from his full participation in the affairs of St John's Church.

LOPPING HALL LIBRARY

We should first mention his role with the Lopping Hall Institute and Reading Room. Lopping Hall had been built in 1884 at a cost of £3,000 which had been funded from the compensation given by the Corporation of London for the relinquishing by the parishioners of Loughton of their ancient lopping rights in Epping Forest. The Hall consisted of two committee rooms, a reading room, library and rooms for the caretaker on the ground floor, and a large assembly room accommodating four to five hundred people and green room on the first floor. The building was in the Gothic style and the architect was Edmund Egan who was a local man known to Waller and who designed several other buildings in Loughton which still exist today.

Living in Loughton with a keen interest in the forest and as an antiquarian and historian it is not surprising that we find that Waller was elected as the Honorary Librarian for the Lopping Hall Library. He appears to have held this position for about ten years and thus saw its development.

An advertisement in the local almanac for 1892 refers to the library containing nearly eighteen hundred standard works on fiction, poetry and history and is open to all parishioners of Loughton above the age of eighteen. There was a subscription (in 1892) of one shilling for three months but, quite rightly, 'Loppers' were free. The library was open on Monday afternoons from 4.00pm to 5.00pm and on Thursday evenings from 8.00pm to 9.00pm. These opening hours did vary in the early years. 'Any further

Circulating Library,

LOUGHTON LOPPING HALL.

The LIBRARY containing nearly eighteen hundred standard Works in Fiction, History, &c., is open, under certain conditions, to all Parishioners of Loughton above the age of Eighteen.

TERMS OF SUBSCRIPTION:
ONE SHILLING FOR THREE MONTHS.
(Loppers Free.)

HOURS OF ATTENDANCE:
MONDAY AFTERNOONS, 4 to 5 O'CLOCK.
THURSDAY EVENINGS, 8 to 9 O'CLOCK.

A new INDEX CATALOGUE, *price* 8*d.*

Any further particulars will be gladly furnished at the Hall, by the Hon. Librarian; to whom also Donations in books or money may be sent. All moneys received, whether by way of Donation or Subscription, are devoted to the purchase of new or repair of old books.

Lists of books added are advertised, from time to time, in the LOUGHTON PARISH MAGAZINE, which is obtainable at both Post Offices, monthly; price 2d.

Circulating Library advertisement

particulars will be gladly furnished at the Hall by the Hon Librarian, to whom all donations in books or money may be sent.'

Another advertisement, this time in the Parish Magazine in March 1890, listed some forty books recently added to the library and included Kipling's *Plain Tales From the Hills,* Jules Verne's *North against South,* and Louis Engel's *From Handel to Halle.*

The library also held a number of volumes on the history of Loughton and Essex and in some cases a note is made that a book is only to be lent out on special resolution of the Trustees. There is an interesting story as to how one such book came to be donated to the library. In 1870 a Commission was set up by Parliament to look into the illegal enclosures of Epping Forest. To assist the Commissioners, the Rolls of the Court of Attachments for the period 1713-1848 were reprinted in 1873. One of the Commissioners was Henry Ford Barclay of Woodford. Following the passing of the Epping Forest Act of 1878 under which the Corporation of London became Conservators of the Forest, and completion of the subsequent arbitration proceedings dealing with the illegal enclosures, Mr Barclay's set (3 volumes) of the Court Rolls was offered to the Essex Field Club. However, they already had a set and that well known figure in the history of the saving of Epping Forest, Edward North Buxton of Knighton, obtained the set and donated them to Lopping Hall Library.

The three volumes, together with the letter from Buxton to Waller as the Honorary Librarian, offering them to the library now reside in the local County library. Lopping Hall Library closed in 1937 but the Hall continues as a venue for local societies such as the Amateur Operatic and Dramatic Societies.

LOUGHTON MUTUAL LABOR-AID SOCIETY

1891 saw the inauguration in Loughton of a social initiative which had a slightly different background to other similar organisations. We have seen Waller's research into the early Huguenot Friendly Societies, the purpose of which was mainly to provide financial support in the event of illness.

The Loughton Mutual Labor-Aid Society, was set up to meet specific needs caused by unemployment among local workers.

The context of the foundation of the Society appears to lie in harsh weather over several years and a depressed economic situation. There is no extant record of the scale of contributions or benefits but the minute book of the Society does record amounts paid in total by members at some meetings. Some better off inhabitants of Loughton were enrolled as honorary members on payment of a lump sum contribution and included the local clergy, local landowners and builders and two solicitors. The money received from these members was paid into a separate fund which was used for purposes other than the relief of unemployment.

Waller was elected President of the Society in March 1891 and remained President until the Society was dissolved in 1899. Although relatively short-lived the Society formed part of the campaign to provide some form of financial security during unemployment, which was to lead to compulsory unemployment insurance introduced by the Government in 1913.

(For a full description of the Society see: 'A social initiative in Loughton, Essex: The Loughton Mutual Labor-Aid Society, 1891-1899, by Edwin Dare, published in the *Local Historian,* November 1994.)

OTHER ORGANISATIONS

In 1909 Waller was appointed a Justice of the Peace, sitting on the Epping Bench. He also sat on the Management Committee of the local Medical Provident Club and was Chairman of the Loughton Horticultural Society, which judging from photographs of their annual show in the early years of the twentieth century, was a well supported organisation.

In 1897 Loughton, in common with all other towns and villages, organised some celebrations for the Diamond Jubilee of Queen Victoria. Waller was a member of the organising Committee and one particular event that he arranged was a bonfire on Baldwins Hill. As this was on Forest land he had to obtain the permission of the

Conservators. The correspondence between Waller, the Superintendent of Epping Forest and the City Solicitor at Guildhall still exists. The Conservators provided some bundles of faggots for the bonfire but somewhat miserly appear to have charged for them. A Fete was also held in the village at which children were provided with a free Tea and the aged and poor received a free Meat Tea.

In March 1908 Waller stood for election as a Verderer of Epping Forest. The existing Verderers for the northern parishes of the Forest were Sir Thomas Fowell Buxton and Waller's friend Peter Gellatly, the local Loughton solicitor. They had decided not to seek re-election and three nominations were put forward to succeed them: Edward North Buxton, Gerald Buxton and William Chapman Waller. The two Buxtons were elected which was not surprising considering their land and property interests throughout the area and the involvement of the family in saving Epping Forest.

Terracotta relief above entrance to Lopping Hall

Wahab's Cottage, Goldings Hill, Loughton, 1903

Pump Hill, Loughton, 1906

12
THE LEGACY

In trying to assess the contribution made by William Chapman Waller to the history of Loughton and Essex, together with his other interests in the community, one aspect which stands out is his attention to detail and the meticulous way in which he recorded everything. This ranges from his translations of manuscripts in Latin to the diaries of his bicycle rides throughout Essex.

A number of Waller's notebooks remain and one has recently come to light. This contains notes on two MSS which Waller studied and are perfect examples of his classical training and attention to detail.

The first document is Earl Spencer's MSS of grants to Waltham Abbey and mainly relates to manors in Hertfordshire. In a preface to his notes Waller says that in December 1892 he had permission to examine these documents at Spencer House. They consisted of a mass of deeds from Edward I to Elizabeth – all in a heap thrown into a box. Waller was at Spencer House, St James's on 1 December from 11.30 to 3.30 and resumed on the 6 and 7 December. On the 14 December he continued operations and finished the exercise on 19 December. The deeds, Waller says, are in fine preservation and a good many still have the seals attached. The ensuing notes, in Waller's neat handwriting, summarise each deed, with some extracts in Latin.

The second set of MSS Waller found in the Cambridge University Library in June 1893. They are of even more interest as they refer to the Courts of Waltham Forest in the time of James I and Charles I. The administrative law of the Forest is described including the appointment of woodwards, regarders and reeves. The collection of charges, presentations, and warrants are explained, with references to the Forest Courts, from the junior Court of Attachments, to the Swainmote and the Court of the Lord Chief Justice in Eyre. Waller used these MSS as one of the sources for his history of Loughton during the seventeenth century.

Waller was fortunate that he did not have to work for a

living but he was extremely industrious in his other activities. Apart from his contribution to the history of Loughton and Essex we must not forget his considerable output, mainly with his great friend William Minet, for the Huguenot Society.

The academic side of his work no doubt took up the major part of his time, but as we have seen the local Church Vestry, the Epping Bench, the Loughton Mutual Labor-Aid Society, the Medical Provident Club and not least the Loughton Horticultural Society all benefited from his knowledge.

Waller's writings in books, transactions of societies and MSS, together with the photographic record are spread around many institutions. In writing this memoir it could be considered the first step in trying to put together a comprehensive archive of all Waller's output in one place, such as the Essex Record Office. At the very least a start could be made on a detailed indexed Bibliography of him

St Mary's Church, Loughton, September 1903

BIBLIOGRAPHY

This list is not intended as a full bibliography. It only refers to works included in this memoir. Waller contributed many other articles, papers and notes to the various organisations of which he was a member. The Essex Record Office also holds some Waller MSS, other than those referred to below.

Abbreviations:

> EAS = The transactions of the *Essex Archaeological Society.*
> EN = *Essex Naturalist,* the transactions of the *Essex Field Club.*
> ER = *Essex Review.*
> *Huguenot Society:* P = Proceedings, QS = Quarto Series
> ERO = *Essex Record Office.*

'Loughton in Essex', *Parish Magazine and 12 bound copies* (1889-1900)
'An Itinerary of Loughton', MS *private collection* (1905-1912)
'Loughton in Essex, a brief account of the Manor and Parish', *published privately,* (1913)
'Monk Wood in Loughton', EN, V (1891) p174
'The old track from London to Epping', EN, VI (1892) p206
'Sake's (commonly Snake's) Lane, Woodford', EN, VI (1892) p208 & VII (1893) p25
'Old Loughton Hall', EN, VII (1893) p14 & p70
'Two Forest Lodges', EN, VII (1893) p82
'Dannetts Hill', EN, VII (1893) p200
'The Epping Hunt', EN, VIII (1894) p31
'The Barclay-Johnston MSS relating to Epping Forest', EN, IX (1895) p157
'Sandpit Plain', EN, VIII (1894) p157
'Ship-Money in Essex 1634-1640', EAS, VIII (1903) p8
'Some account of the church of St Nicholas at Loughton', EAS, XIV (1918) p275
'A note on the Hundred of Ongar', EAS, IX (1906) p212
'A fourteenth century Pluralist: Richard de Drax, Rector of Harlow', EAS, XII (1913) p291
'An extinct county family: Wroth of Loughton Hall', EAS, VIII (1903) p145 & 345, and IX (1906) p1
'Friday Hill and the Boothbys', EAS, XIII (1915) p113
'Some additions to Newcourt's Repertorium', EAS, VI (1898) p126, p228, p298,VII (1900) p153, p272, p356, X (1909) p312, XIII (1915) p144
'Essex Field Names', EAS, V (1895) p144, VI (1898) p60, p258, VII (1900) p65, p285, VIII (1903) p76, p199, p295, IX (1906) p68
'Court Rolls of manors of Wethersfield and Wivenhoe', EAS, X (1909) p246, p320
'Inventories of church goods', EAS, XI (1911) p310

'Old Chigwell wills' EAS, X (1909) p237, XI (1911) p10, p150, p335
'Feet of Fines', EAS, XII (1913) p193
'Obituary', EAS XIV (1918) p356
'The Foresters Walks in Waltham Forest', ER, XIV (1905) p193
'An Essex Alchemist', ER, XIII (1904) p19
'Luxborough in Chigwell', ER, XIV (1905) p1
'The Abbots of Waltham in the Papal Registers', ER, XXI (1912) p151
'Historical note on Monkhams', ER, XIV (1905) p167
'The Deer in Waltham Forest 1588-1591', ER, XV (1906) p61 & 140
'Some ancient charities', ER, XV (1906) p179
'Early Huguenot Friendly Societies', *Huguenot Society,* P VI p265
''The Protestant church at Guisnes', *Huguenot Society,* QS III (1891)
'The French church known as La Patente in Spittlefields', *Huguenot Society,* QS XI (1898)
'The French church at Thorpe-le-Soken', *Huguenot Society,* QS XX (1912)
'Dutch church at Colchester', *Huguenot Society,* QS XII (1905)
'Extracts from Weavers' Company', *Huguenot Society,* QS XXXIII (1931)
'Waller archive', ERO:

>Ref D/P 233/7/3 Papers relating to Consistory Court
>Ref D/P 233/8/3 Vestry minutes 1869-1908
>Ref D/P 233/28/22 Receipt from Harvard College
>Ref D/P 233/25/19 Benefactions to parish of Loughton
>Ref D/P 233/28/15 Account of St John's Church
>Ref T/P 2/1 Notebooks (14), rough notes used in preparation of *Loughton in Essex*
>Ref T/R 19/1 Transcript of Loughton parish registers
>Ref T/M 89/1 Map of parish of Loughton c 1820
>Ref T/P 13/1 'Odds and Ends' – 7 volumes of notes and newspaper cuttings – 1890-1917

INDEX

Forest pool